THE NO-NONSENSE LANDLORD

BUILDING WEALTH
WITH
RENTAL PROPERTIES

THE
NO-NONSENSE
LANDLORD

BUILDING WEALTH
WITH
RENTAL PROPERTIES

RICHARD H. JORGENSEN

LIBERTY HOUSE®

This publication is designed to provide accurate and authoritative information in regard to the subject matter covered. It is sold with the understanding that the publisher is not engaged in rendering legal, accounting or other professional service. If legal advice or other expert assistance is required, the services of a competent professional person should be sought.

FROM A DECLARATION OF PRINCIPLES JOINTLY ADOPTED BY A COMMITTEE OF THE AMERICAN BAR ASSOCIATION AND A COMMITTEE OF PUBLISHERS.

LIBERTY HOUSE books are published by LIBERTY HOUSE, a division of TAB BOOKS Inc. Its trademark, consisting of the words "LIBERTY HOUSE" and the portrayal of Benjamin Franklin, is registered in the United States Patent and Copyright Office.

FIRST EDITION
FIRST PRINTING

Library of Congress Cataloging-in-Publication Data

Jorgensen, Richard H.
    The no-nonsense landlord : building wealth with rental properties
    / by Richard H. Jorgensen.
      p. cm.
    Includes index.
    ISBN 0-8306-9032-8
    1. Rental housing. 2. Real estate investment. I. Title.
HD1394.J67 1988
332.63'243—dc 19
                          88-25088
                          CIP

TAB BOOKS Inc. offers software for sale. For information and a catalog, please contact TAB Software Department, Blue Ridge Summit, PA 17294-0850.

Questions regarding the content of this book should be addressed to:

Reader Inquiry Branch
TAB BOOKS Inc.
Blue Ridge Summit, PA 17294-0214

To My Good Friend

Roger Rook

Who Provided Me with the Inspiration
And to My Friends and Associates

Lois Henkel

Mary Haynes

Marilyn Oelke

Sandy Walker

Who Gave Me the Freedom to
Complete This Project

Contents

Considerate of the Tenant Can Be Costly • Charge the Proper Rent • Dispel the Cadillac Image with Your Tenants • The Meaning of Tenant Leases

THE
NO-NONSENSE
LANDLORD

BUILDING WEALTH
WITH
RENTAL PROPERTIES

Introduction

AS I'VE LOOKED BACK OVER MY CAREER IN THE REAL ESTATE BUSINESS, I've come to the realization that I've experienced a great deal of personal satisfaction, along with a fair amount of financial success. Because the business has been good to me, I believe it's only right that I contribute something back in exchange.

The way I figure it, there's no better way for any one of us to make a contribution than to give of those things we know best. After all, what good does it do if we acquire special knowledge, develop unique talents, and accumulate years of experience if we do not pass on this valuable information for others to use?

What I have to offer is this book, which is filled with real-life experiences taken from my years of investing in real estate. In addition, there are success stories told to me by reliable investors.

The primary theme of this book is to show how ordinary people, just like you and me, can invest in real estate and accumulate wealth. Throughout the book there's a constant flow of positive, thought-provoking ideas about real estate investing. This message will produce assurance that anyone—the average everyday person, those with an entrepreneurial spirit—can take that first step and buy investment property. There's a further message, repeated over and over, telling the average person how important it is to establish financial security. That's something we all strive for. There's convincing evidence in this book that you can achieve it through real estate investing.

The book literally is filled with "how-to" information and packed with practical, common-sense, down-to-earth methods of selecting profitable properties, choosing good tenants, collecting rents, handling complaints, and managing the everyday details of a successful real estate operation.

Also, there's ample information on how to buy, finance, own, and manage properties with a minimum of hardships, difficulties, and anxieties. There's advice on how to eliminate some of the headaches encountered in the rental business.

In plain language, this book tells how to cut costs of operations— how to use shrewd, smart, and even some cheapskate methods of buying and maintaining properties.

You might ask, "What's the big deal? There are plenty of real estate books out there. What have you got to say that's so different?"

My response to that is simply this: This book is different from other real estate books because there are no get-rich-quick schemes, no pie-in-the-sky theory, and no quick-fix proposals for real estate investing. This book is a realistic and constructive guide to buying, owning, and managing investment property. The book is best defined by a friend of mine who said, "This is a book about the real world of real estate."

I know the real estate business. I've been in it for 24 years. During that time I've had to solve problems through trial and error. My ideas have worked well for me, and I think they're worth passing on.

I wish I would have had a real estate book like this when I first started in the business. It could have saved me a lot of time, trouble, mistakes, and headaches, as well as some financial losses. That's hindsight investing, however, and we can't operate any business on hindsight—but we can learn from other people's experiences.

My theory of business is not only based on the 24 years of experience I have, but on an accumulation of life's experiences. These experiences have ingrained some of the traits I've adopted over the years. In this book I will tell you about some of them.

I'm not telling you the following story to impress you with my accomplishments, but to let you know that if I can do it, anyone can.

My beginnings were indeed humble. I come from a very poor background—at least financially speaking. My grandparents raised me in a small rural village back in the 1930s and 1940s.

There might have been one or two families in our community who were poorer, but we certainly were among the poorest. Of course, in those days most of us only knew poor. It was difficult to relate to any other way of life, and it was totally incomprehensible to relate to money, wealth, and riches.

I knew there were better things out there, though, and I wanted them. I was sure of one thing: if I did want them I could only depend on myself to get them. That meant if I was going to reach any sort of goal, I had to take my own destiny in hand. It was the start of what we might call "survival instinct."

In order to start on the road to success, I knew I'd have to develop some affirmative action—or more bluntly, I'd have to become pushy and assertive. This development was the beginning of the assertiveness I've used in my real estate business. You'll hear more about it as we go.

As a young person I was on the outside looking in, and had a very limited view of what wealth meant. I fantasized what people with money did—go to college, travel, self-employed, and live what seemed to be a life of luxury. Those fantasies were great and frankly were important in my overall character development. They contributed to my bold determination to succeed.

Over the years other characteristics emerged. I certainly learned to be miserly. I had to in order to survive. Each hard-earned penny was important because it was hard to come by.

The economic world and value system on the outside seemed much different for those who were more fortunate and had money. For instance, when starting poor, a person tends to be much more conservative about spending, especially squandering. Also, you develop a self-protectionism and become more defensive when someone wants what's yours. You might call it "thrift awareness." My friends tell me it's being a cheapskate. Either way it's all right with me. I know it works. In fact, those are the reasons I've been a shrewd manager with my finances—which, of course, includes real estate. My experiences revealed to me how important environment plays in developing a person's self esteem and self worth. Guilt feelings and self doubt are all formulated during our growing years. Sometimes they're hard to overcome.

Although you've read and heard about people getting rich quick in real estate, I can't tell you of any get-rich-quick schemes. I don't know any secret formulas or easy ways to real estate wealth. I didn't become a millionaire overnight, and I didn't get rich by attending real estate seminars. I can't make you rich. I don't have any gimmicks or tricks, no 24-hour schemes that work. As a matter of fact, in my case, it took more like 24 years to accumulate the property and develop it into a profitable, viable, and successful business.

It seems a little dishonest and deceptive to tell anyone they can get rich quick in real estate—or any other business for that matter.

Not only did it take that much time to acquire the property, but it took a lot of time to learn the necessary management skills to make the property run smoothly.

Now, if you're willing to accept this, then this book, which is an accumulation of my experiences, should help you establish a real estate business in less time than it took me, with a lot less trial-and-error methods of operation. This book contains no frills, no wild-eyed ideas, and no concoction that's not realistic and workable. This book doesn't deal with any "snake oil" cure for real estate problems. There's no secret formula or step-by-step plan of action to acquire immediate success and wealth. So, what this book is then, is a practical, down-to-earth, straight-from-the-shoulder common sense, plain-talking, everyday, hard-working, no-nonsense approach to positive real estate ownership and management.

Getting rich in real estate my way might not be as quick as you've been led to believe, but the property will always be there. It's certainly one of the best ways I know of to establish savings and security, and that savings will be as solid as the Rock of Gibraltar.

It's my hope that your journey through this book will be as enjoyable and fulfilling for you to read as it has been for me to write. Now, let's get on with the story.

1

The Future of Real Estate Is as Solid as the Rock of Gibraltar

ALL OF US AT ONE TIME OR ANOTHER HAVE THOUGHT ABOUT BUYING IN-vestment property, but few of us have taken that initial step and made the first investment. This hesitation seems especially true for those of us who weren't born into money, who didn't inherit money, and us who literally started our business and investment career from scratch.

With this fact in mind, I knew that I'd have to find a way to convince you of a well-known fact, and that is: anyone can invest in real estate. However, very few of us do buy and own investment property. That's probably why about 10 percent of the people own and control 90 percent of the wealth in this country. I can't change that, and I don't think I can get you into the 10 percent group right way. However, I can show you a plan that can get you started in the real estate investment business.

To start, let me tell you that real estate represents one of the most powerful and dynamic businesses there is, and there's plenty of evidence to prove this statement. In fact, this book is filled with the proof. Let me start by pointing out the following:

- Many investors experience positive things in real estate, like building a viable independent business without investing a great deal of money.
- Many small investors experience the *personal satisfaction* of buying property and watching it develop into a good investment and profitable venture.

• Many investors experience untold *success stories* with all the *financial benefits* related to buying property, such as building a stable net worth and developing a substantial rental income.

• Many investors started with one property, experienced success, and then went on to bigger and better investments.

• Real estate investments represent one of the best ways to establish *financial security*.

LOOK TO REAL ESTATE FOR FINANCIAL SECURITY

Financial security is as important as any other phase of investing—one that's sold me and should sell you. Most of us spend our working lives looking for financial security. It's something that's not all that easy to come by. It seems like some of us work all our lives and end up with a pension and gold watch, while others might not be quite so lucky and need to depend on social security.

I've found that real estate is one of the best vehicles there is for financial independence. It's not elusive; it's something that's totally dependable; it can't be taken away; and it's security that's literally as solid as the Rock of Gibraltar. There's nothing more comforting to the body and soul than financial security.

REAL ESTATE REMAINS SECURE

When I say there's solid financial security with real estate, there's plenty of evidence to prove this statement. For instance, over the years we've seen both good and bad economic times. There has been turbulance in our economic system—some call them recessions or depressions. As everyone knows, there've been many business failures and record bankruptcies, not to mention the erratic action of the stock market.

Despite all the economic disruptive forces, real estate remains basically stable and secure. That fact indicates, other than with a few exceptions, that there has never been a dramatic decrease in the value of real estate. In fact, most of the time there has been appreciation, and that's what is meant by *real estate security*: good, basic, solid value for the dollar invested.

There are failures in real estate. Some people ask, "If real estate's so great, why do I hear about all these people who've bought property and gone broke?" They might even mention how the bottom fell out of the Houston real estate market, as well as other distressed areas and locations.

Yes, I agree. All these failures have happened and most likely will continue to happen. The reason I say they will continue is because some very obvious and basic weaknesses exist that have caused the failures. Real estate itself has not caused them. Here's what I mean.

Greed can be as devastating as cheating. Quick bucks, easy money, and get-rich-quick schemes all represent questionable business tactics. How often have we heard about someone who has been taken by some slick salesman, hot stocks, oil wells, nothing-down deals, and "you can't go wrong" gimmicks? Caution!

Many investors have become greedy and invested in some get-rich-quick schemes. Others bought property at highly inflated prices, got heavily in debt, couldn't make the payments, didn't know what the future represented for their investment, and lost everything.

Some investors, including some of the rich and famous, became over-zealous and just kept buying regardless of the circumstances. Others invested, then mismanaged their property. They didn't pay attention to the costs of operation until they got into severe financial difficulty. They ended up with mortgages and payments they couldn't handle and ultimately a financial sinkhole. Other investors lived a lavish life-style off their real estate income before paying the bills, and literally went bankrupt because of it.

We all have heard about these failures, know they exist, and even have seen some of them on the evening news.

USE COMMON SENSE

We all have a job or business—something most of us have to do. There's nothing wrong with having a job, but the trouble is that it takes a lot of time and energy. I'm sure most of us are paid well for what we do, but the sad part of the job or business is that we invest all that time and energy and there's never any money left over. We all earn plenty, but the odds are pretty good that we spend most of what we make. I know. I've been there. We work more, make more, and along comes an increase in life-style—I mean like new cars, new boats, new and bigger homes, etc. At the end of the year, we sit back and ask ourselves, "Where did all the money go? There's nothing left in savings. I'm trying to build some security."

If you see this situation happening in your life, it might be time to look to real estate. All those trappings might represent the great American dream story, but it seems to be no more than a dream with a rude awakening.

Most assuredly, investors who've gone beyond their means don't represent the "good and successful investor"—the ones who make it. Many stories exist about the "good and successful investor"—those investors who used common business sense, who invested wisely, who lived within their means, who managed their property well, who didn't try to keep up with the Joneses and who didn't expect to become rich overnight. You know something? They're still around, and doing quite well.

Those good and successful investors are not only still around, but they're becoming wealthy—maybe not as quickly as we might have been led to believe by the quick-fix deals, but they are becoming real-estate rich. Those are the capable, thinking, successful investors you'll be reading about in this book. Those good and successful investors aren't all that visible. You don't read about them everyday or see them on television, but they're there. I believe that their advice, which is dispersed throughout this book, should add greatly to your ability to get started and succeed in the real estate business.

YOU DON'T HAVE TO BE
A FINANCIAL WIZARD TO SUCCEED

Most of those good and successful investors who are buying real estate in today's market and getting rich are people just like you and me. I know them and have met many of them. They're people who have used their "smarts" to get where they are. They know that the real estate business is a business where you can use your brain power and do very well. I'm convinced that part of their success can be attributed to good old common sense.

A fellow investor told me once, "The way I see it, if you learn the business, use common sense, and know your 'stuff,' you can operate a real estate investment business with about 95 percent mental participation and about 5 percent physical work." I believe him; he's right. It's not necessary to be a "Wall Street Whiz Kid" and you don't need a lot of MBA degrees to succeed in this business. All you need is a little more than average intelligence and a lot of common sense.

Not only can you invest in real estate by using common sense, but it's not at all necessary to be wealthy. The smart real estate investor uses his thinking power, borrows other people's money (the bankers), and pays off the investment mortgage with other people's money (the tenants). Other people's money pays off the mortgage and builds equity. Equity represents one of the most profound and secure savings there is.

Add to the equity advantage another advantage of real estate investing called *appreciation,* which is the increase in value of the property. Appreciation also represents savings and security. That's why I say, real estate represents one of the best ways there is to establish financial security.

Most good and successful investors know that equity and appreciation are virtually risk free. It's almost like a perpetual money machine: a machine that works every day, both day and night, vacations, and at all times. It is The Great American Dream come true.

Let me point out something significant. In order to succeed in this business, in order to make sure there is appreciation and equity, it takes good, sound management practices. I don't want to make it sound so easy that management is overlooked. It shouldn't be. Managerial skills are important. A good manager will always have:

- A good, positive attitude
- A keen eye on expenses
- An assertive and aggressive attitude in business dealings
- A lot of plain old common sense
- Old-fashioned ideas that work

A Positive Attitude Will Make Positive Things Happen

I can't say enough about the importance of a positive attitude, positive thinking, and positive management. It's important to the success of the real estate business, or any other business for that matter. For this reason I have devoted Chapter 15 to positive thinking.

Keep a Keen Eye on Expenses

Along with positive thinking, you need some shrewd financial skills to run a real estate business. What I mean, and this will be pointed out throughout the book, is that it takes some shrewd, tightwad, and yes even some cheapskate methods of buying, owning, operating, and managing real estate.

You've probably heard of the late J. Paul Getty of Getty Oil, who was at one time one of the wealthiest people in the world. Not only did he have millions of dollars, along with a considerable amount of investment property, but he owned a large country estate in England.

Over the years, Getty discovered that some of his guests would make long-distance telephone calls from his mansion in England and never pay for the calls. Do you know what he did, and justifiably so? He installed a pay telephone in the mansion. This pay telephone eliminated the long-distance telephone bills. That's shrewd management. Some might call it being a tightwad; I call it being a practical cheapskate. This example is the kind of cheapskate tactics I'll advocate throughout this book.

Management also calls for some penny pinching and tightening of the purse strings when it comes to cutting costs of operation. Learning to know where the money comes from and where it goes is called *bean counting*. Let me tell you, bean counting makes profits.

Because we've lost some of the tax benefits we've had, we must take extra care to squeeze out the profits. We've also lost that built-in, fast-action inflation we've experienced over the years (although I have a feeling that loss will be short lived).

Actually, all this means that real estate investing is now in a position it should have been all along. It depends on management to make the project work and make profits.

Real estate investors of the past have found it pretty much an "easy come, easy go" proposition. You really didn't have to do a lot of shrewd bean counting to make the business succeed and ensure profits. The new changes, however, have made the real estate business more dependent on sound fiscal management.

Success Demands Assertive and Aggressive Management

In addition to being tight with the financial reigns, today's manager must be assertive and aggressive in making business decisions and dealing with his tenants, employees, contractors, sellers, and bankers. It's not necessary to become a scoundrel, a slum landlord or a money grubber. It's merely a matter of letting the people with whom you deal know you mean business.

Common-Sense Management is the Best Management

As I've said, it takes common-sense management to succeed. I can tell you from my own experience—and I think most investors will tell you the same thing—that to be successful in the real estate business is a matter of using common-sense, down-to-earth, practical methods of buying, financially managing, and caring for a property. What this statement means is that we should eliminate problems before they occur. Eliminating problems before they occur can and will make life easier and will develop a more financially secure business. The result will provide peace of mind.

2

How to Get Started in the Real Estate Business

DESPITE ALL MY ENTHUSIASM AND ALL THE REAL ESTATE SUCCESS STOR-
ies, I have a hard time convincing people that *now* is a good time, in fact
the best time there is, to buy real estate.

Some of the excuses I've heard from those who haven't made up
their mind and taken that first step toward buying are:

- Time just isn't right.
- There's too much financial turmoil out there.
- There's not enough stability in our economic system.
- There's going to be a depression.
- I don't want to lose my money.
- I don't want to go broke.

These excuses aren't new; they've been around for years. For me they
just don't hold water. I'm convinced that now is the best time to buy
investment property, and I can prove it.

In all my years of investing in rental property, I've never experienced
unrest, failure, or a decline in values of real estate. I could have said
this yesterday, 1 year ago, or 5 years ago and I will continue saying that
until I'm proven wrong.

The fact is that tax reform doesn't mean you can't make money in
investment real estate. Owning investment property makes sound financial
sense despite the new tax laws. I say this because there's no doubt that,
over the long run, property that's well cared for and properly managed
almost always increases in value—and usually faster than overall inflation.

Add to that the fact that the new tax law hasn't changed the fact that real estate taxes, mortgage interest, depreciation, and the cost of operation are all fully tax deductible.

I can make this statement and back it up: I've been investing in real estate for years, through thick and thin, in good times and bad, and I've never had a property do anything but appreciate in value. With that same property, during that same period of time, the rents have appreciated accordingly. Also, as everyone in the real estate business knows, as rents go, so goes the value of property.

Let me add one more thing. I've never had any vacancies of consequences, and no loss of income, and I've *never* made a bad investment. Some were better than others, but none were bad.

Some of the skeptics will tell you that the glory days of investing in real estate are over. Not so. I'm convinced that another surge of inflation is just around the corner. Inflation is money in the bank for the real estate investor.

The point is, get started *now*. Be optimistic and positive. There's a bright future out there in real estate. You might say, ''That's easy for you to say. You've already made yours.'' That isn't the case, because I could have said the same thing 5, 10, or 15 years ago, as well as yesterday and today.

I've heard some comments like, ''Yeah, but when you bought your property it was cheaper.'' That's true, but rents were cheaper, so was lumber, hardware, labor, and everything else. As a matter of fact, I didn't buy all my property ''back then.'' I buy property all the time and just bought a duplex this past year—and intend to continue buying.

Once you get in the run of things there's no reason you can't handle and buy one property a year.

DON'T LET EXCUSES GET IN THE WAY

It's easy to find excuses not to buy property. In fact, excuses will eliminate any possibility of taking a chance.

Excuse makers become procrastinators. They don't have to make decisions. Conversely, they don't make much progress, and for sure, they don't make much money. I like to have procrastinators around. They don't get in the way and make it difficult for those of us who want to get things done. Procrastinators certainly narrow down the competition.

———————

There are a lot of unique opportunities out there. Start looking now.

———————

OVERCOME THE HINDSIGHT MILLIONAIRE SYNDROME

Most procrastinators will find excuses like:

"Boy, if I'd bought that property back in 1970 when prices were right, but now I don't know."
or,

"I should have bought that 10 acres in Hawaii in 1960."
and,

"Do you know that I looked at that apartment building once and could have bought it for $165,000, and now it's selling for $245,000?"

These kinds of people don't get going and don't make much money.

We're all excellent hindsight millionaires, but the smart investor doesn't look back and think of what he could have done 10 or 15 years ago. The good and successful, and I might add smart, investor starts *now* and looks ahead.

PROCRASTINATORS DON'T BECOME MILLIONAIRES

From what I've seen in the real estate world, and from talking to various people over the years, the odds are pretty good that the average person will not buy real estate, other than his or her personal home. The odds are even better that the same person won't become a millionaire. Do you know why? Because most people can't make decisions.

Despite all the pep talks, regardless of our good intentions, it's not all that easy to go out and buy that first property—or second, or third for that matter. It's quite a step for most of us to take. It can be awesome for some of us. There's no doubt it creates some anxieties. Don't despair, though, and don't become overly anxious. Anyone can buy real estate today. It's like anything else in life that's good: it takes some motivation to get started. It's a matter of taking the plan from the thinking and dreaming stage to the acting on it stage.

Some people have gone so far as to buy real estate books. They've read through them, convinced themselves that they can do it, and become temporarily motivated. They truly believe they are going to get started, but then they wait—just a little. That stall usually leads to waiting too long, though. The motivation is short-lived. They put the books away, go back to their daily routine, and pretty much forget everything. The next thing you know the other person bought the duplex or the apartment they had their eye on.

Three types of people exist. Those who:

- Get things done and make things happen
- Watch things happen
- Ask "What happened?"

That's enough on that. Now, let's get on to buying property, and learning the trade.

THERE'S NO SECRET FORMULA
IN DETERMINING A GOOD BUY

I wish I could tell you exactly and precisely how to determine a fair and marketable price for real estate. I don't have such a formula, and in all the years I've been in real estate I've never found anyone who does. The only surefire way I know how to buy right is to get a good real estate education, take your time, and know what you're doing.

There are some basic questions you can answer before starting. For example:

- Can I afford the property?
- Will the income cover the expenses?
- How can I recognize a good deal?
- Do I like it?
- Is it in a good location?
- How can I deal with the seller?

Can I Afford the Property?

First, know your own finances and determine what you can afford to pay. Don't look at property that's not within your financial ability. If you're only in a position to buy a duplex or four-plex, there's no sense in looking at a 24-unit apartment building.

Next, start small. Buy something within your means. Get one property started and making a profit, then look for the next property.

I'm sure I don't have to tell you that every community has it's own values for real estate. Obviously real estate has a different value in San Francisco, California, than in Clear Lake, Iowa.

Even though prices are different in different locations, some factors exist that cover both San Francisco as well as Clear Lake, Iowa. For instance:

- Is there sufficient income to cover the costs of operation?
- Is the property overpriced?

If the investment isn't going to make financial sense, if the income is not sufficient to cover the costs, or if the property is too high, then it's obviously not a good investment.

Determining Price is Difficult

I can't tell you the prices of property in Clear Lake or San Francisco, but I can tell you that in my location I've paid from about $15,000 to $20,000 per unit in a multiple dwelling, older apartment building. These figures mean a six-plex in my area will cost about $120,000. These figures also mean I need to receive about $350 per month rent to maintain a positive cash flow.

On the other hand, $120,000 won't buy a stick in San Francisco or New York. In addition, you can't look at any rental unit in these cities for under $1,000 per month. To make a determination of whether property is a good buy or not, ask these questions:

- Is there sufficient income to cover the costs?
- If the income isn't there, should I use my own money?
- Do I have a personal or business cash reserve that can be used to cover an emergency?

Let's answer these one at a time.

Is There Sufficient Income? Does the Property Have a Positive Cash Flow? Positive *Cash flow* means having enough income to cover all the expenses. To better understand, let's take a hypothetical investment property. We'll use a $100,000 property with a 25-year mortgage at 9 percent interest. Following is the cost of that property:

Mortgage payment	$827
Taxes	$150
Utilities	$150
Maintenance, repair	$120
Advertising	$ 10
Insurance	$ 50
Garbage	$ 15
Soft Water	$ 24
Misc. expenses	$ 50

The total expenses are $1,346.98, which means it takes that amount of rent income for the property to have a positive cash flow. If it doesn't have a positive cash flow, the next question is, where does the money come from?

Should I Use My Own Personal Money? Eventually you will be faced with the question, should I use my personal money to buy and invest in real estate, or can I depend on borrowed money and nothing down deals? I can't answer that for you. There is one thing I can say, however: there's no better place in the world to put your money for secure savings than in real estate!

What About A Cash Reserve? Sometimes you'll run into situations that will demand more money, whether you want to spend it or not. For instance, the property might need a new furnace, the building might need to be painted; the building might need some major renovation; or, a good deal could come up that you didn't expect. It could be, if you're like most of us, that you'll be faced with no reserve cash, insufficient rental income to cover the expenses, and no inheritance in the near future (that near future represents about 400 years for me). As a result it will take personal income to cover the expenses. The question is, "Should I take a chance?" Again, I can't answer this question. It is something that only you can determine. You should know that this is a fact of real estate investing.

How to Recognize a Good Deal

Some concerns all investors have are as follows:

- Did I get a good deal?
- Did I pay too much?
- Should I have haggled more on the price?
- Could I have bought the property cheaper?
- Did I act too quickly?
- Was the price right?

In answer to all these questions, there's only one answer, and that is: if it's good for you, then it's a good investment! Leave it at that. Once you've made the decision, don't look back. Whatever you do, don't worry about what other people think. Make a point of not discussing your business with other people. What you paid for your property is your business. Most importantly, if you think it's a good property and you're comfortable with it, then it's a good deal.

Another question investors often ask is, "Do I like it?" If you do, and if you can afford it and you know you can manage it, then it's the right property for you. Regardless of what anyone else says, if it's good for you, it's good—that's all that matters.

Life itself is a chance. You really never know what is going to happen. I know this, though: as far as the odds of getting a bad deal in real estate are concerned, real estate far outweighs the next best investment for security.

Don't be concerned that someone you know might say, "You paid too much for the property, it's not a good deal." It's none of their business.

One final word on this subject. If you're the entrepreneurial type, you know that every investment, whether it's real estate or any other business, is somewhat of a chance. I wouldn't worry too much about real estate, however.

Controlling Your Investment

There are a number of things you can control when buying real estate. The first is location. Buy investment property in a location you like. Especially buy in the same town, community, or city where you live. Buy where you can see your investment everyday.

Don't think the grass is greener on the other side of town or in another city. If you're satisfied that your community is stable or growing, and if you're happy and intend to spend most of your life there, or at least a number of years, then that's the best place to sink your roots and start an investment program in real estate. Another factor you have complete control over is this: don't buy high-priced property in a low-priced neighborhood; buy low-priced property in a high-priced neighborhood. This fact only makes sense. The high-priced property in a low-priced neighborhood is going to depreciate, while low-priced property in a high-priced neighborhood (with good care and upkeep) is bound to appreciate.

Selecting Your Community

Here's something to think about when you're making plans for investments. If you're going to spend your time and money on real estate, you might as well buy in a community that has a good future. If you can see shortcomings, if the community isn't growing, if industry is failing, if there's not a good employment base, and if the community isn't going to make progress, your chances of success diminish.

Also, don't start buying investment property if you're not ready to settle in any particular community. Wait until you expect to live in a particular community for a number of years. Absentee ownership of real estate can be devastating and a loser. It's certainly something I don't recommend.

Here are some other things to consider when choosing a community:

- Is the community growing?
- Is there good education facilities?
- Is there a good solid financial base?
- Is the tax structure stable?

In addition to the community, what is the neighborhood like?

- Is it a quality neighborhood?
- Is it zoned for business and industry?
- Are there traffic and freeway problems?
- Are streets in good repair?
- What's the crime situation in the community?
- Is there any problem with flooding?

What is the property like?

- Is it a low-priced property in a high-priced area?
- Is it a solid, stable building?

Once you've established your territory, know where you intend to live, and know the community and neighborhood, the next step is to deal with the seller.

How to Deal with the Seller

There's no reason to be intimidated by a seller or real estate agent. Put yourself in charge right from the start. Establish your dominance. (Remember; I stressed the importance of being assertive. Now's the time!)

Here's a list of realtor's sales pitch comments you'll hear:

- This is really a good deal that's going to make money.
- This deal isn't going to last so we'd better sign an earnest-money contract right away.
- Why don't you give me $1,000 to hold the property?
- You'd better buy now or someone else will grab it.
- If you don't sign a purchase agreement, I don't know if I can get it passed at this low price.

- You can't go wrong.
- It's a deal you can't pass up.

Sometimes these salespeople act like we've got an IQ of about 65.

Life is too short to go through this hassle. I cut off the communication and let the realtor know I want the truth and I don't need any special sales pitch.

Don't be intimidated by the seller. Keep the door open for communication because the next step is negotiating on *your* terms.

HAGGLE ON THE PRICE

Nobody pays the starting price. Once the price is established, the next move is up to you. Offer 25 percent less than the asking price. Don't be embarrassed about doing so. Don't think you'll look foolish if you do make this offer, and again don't be intimidated by the seller.

You're not in the real estate investment business to make friends; you're in it to make money. If you're going to make money, you're going to have to be an assertive negotiator. Remember, at the beginning of this book I said you're going to have to buy, own, and manage real estate as a "cheapskate." Now's the time to begin.

The cheapskate buyer is the one who ends up with the good deals. Nice guys who are afraid to negotiate and haggle are the ones who end up with high-priced investments—or no investment at all.

THE DUPLEX IS THE BEST STARTER INVESTMENT

If you don't have a lot of money, if you're trying to buy something you can afford and something within your means, if you need housing for yourself, if you're looking for rental income, and if you've made up your mind that *now* is the right time to start an investment program, then my advice is think duplex.

It doesn't make sense to look at a 200-unit apartment building when you can only afford a duplex. If you think too big, you might not get started. On the other hand, it's smart to think big, but think common sense.

The duplex represents the greatest advantages for real estate investment because the duplex is:

- Investment property
- Your own home
- Financially feasible to buy
- An income-producer to pay off the mortgage
- A tax write-off
- Practical and makes sense

Duplexes are readily available to purchase. Not only can you buy one easily, but when you're ready to sell, they sell just as easily.

The duplex is easy to finance. Because you live in the property, government loans are practical. Most loaning agencies look well at the duplex for investment.

With the duplex, you live in one unit and rent out the other. The tenant helps pay off the mortgage. The duplex is 50 percent investment property. That means 50 percent of all expenses are totally tax deductible.

A DUPLEX IS PRACTICAL

My daughter rented an apartment in a large city for a number of years. Then we—she and I—came to our senses, and discovered that by her buying a duplex she paid less (with the tenant's rent) rent living in her own property than renting. Not only that, but it's a larger apartment with a garage—something she didn't have before.

Look for a good, stable duplex located in a residential area. One that needs some repair makes a good investment because the work you do will increase its value.

Move into one of the units, then start remodeling the other. This remodeling can easily be done while it's occupied so there's rental income. The cost of improvements is deductible because this is investment property.

After you have finished remodeling the unit, then move into it and rent out the other half. Start the process again. The remodeling again is tax deductible.

The next step you take could and should be another duplex. Then start the process over. In order to make big money in the real estate business, you will need to own more than one or two properties. I don't mean to say that a duplex won't make money—it will—but I'm talking about getting into the big-money real estate business.

Use common sense, though. Buy within your means. Don't go overboard and end up with payments you can't handle.

WHAT TO LOOK FOR IN A DUPLEX

Figures 2-1 and 2-2 are examples of investment properties that have potential for growth. These two properties, each quite different, represents different types of investments. One is fairly new, in good condition, and considered middle-class housing. The other is older, has less income, but also can be purchased more reasonably.

The first duplex is in good condition. It's located in an excellent neighborhood so there are no deteriorating factors. It's very *rentable* which means it has steady and stable income.

Fig. 2-1. A duplex has all the practical aspects of a starter investment. It is relatively small, which makes it affordable, and is compact, with a garage for each unit. Some minor rejuvenation work is needed, which will increase the value of the property with minimal costs.

The interior has been kept well. There's good oak woodwork throughout; the carpet is in good condition. The kitchens and bathrooms are in good order. Each unit has a garage which is a great selling point for potential tenants.

Some cosmetic repairs need to be made to bring the property up to high quality value. For instance, you can see there's one shutter missing. Also, the small garage doors are shabby and need to be repaired or replaced. In the near future the building will need to be painted. These are jobs that a novice investor can do with no trouble. These jobs, which are simple and represent a minimum of cost, time, and work, can be done on weekends and vacations. The owner probably has ignored the problems. It's kind of like how the old saying goes, "if it works, why fix it." With a few dollars invested, this property could easily represent many dollars in appreciation.

The financial picture of this property looks pretty good. The income is $7,560. Expenses are minimal because everything is paid by the tenants—heat, utilities, garbage, soft water, and lawn service. After deducting the insurance, taxes, and maintenance, there's a net gross

Fig. 2-2. This kind of property is made for a rejuvenation investor. Because it's stucco, the exterior will remain basically maintenance free. This property is a small, very compact, two-bedroom duplex. Because of its size, rents can remain reasonable. Therefore, you should experience no vacancies and a profitable investment if purchased right.

income of $5,574 or $464 per month. This figure means that a 9 percent, 25-year mortgage would pay off the property at a selling price of $57,000. These figures do not consider tax depreciation.

This property obviously costs more than $57,000. Again, I remind you that the location, community, city, or neighborhood can have a dramatic effect on the price of the property, as well as the cost of operation.

So if the property costs more than $57,000, what can be done? First, the investor can take some of his own money and make part of the payment. If renting, the investor can move into the duplex and use his rent money to make the mortgage payment.

Secondly, the rents could be increased to help cover the cost of operation. This increase could be dangerous, however. If the rents are too high, the tenants could move out. Vacancies for an investor who needs the income to pay off the mortgage can be a nightmare.

Thirdly, the payments on the mortgage could be lowered by extending the time to 30 or 35 years. Fourthly, the investor could negotiate a contract for deed purchase with a payment of $464 per month, with a balloon payment at the end of the contract.

The second photograph shows a slightly different kind of investment. This investment is a small duplex, that is compact and, in good condition. It makes an excellent starter investment. Here's the financial history of the property.

The total income (remember location) is $5,160 per year. Expenses include taxes, insurance, and repair: a total of $1,691. The income less expenses leaves a net gross profit of $3,769. A 25-year, 9 percent contract for deed break-even purchase price is $32,000, which means there would be a mortgage payment of $314.00 per month.

This property is a good investment property. It's a good starter and a good investment with great potential for growth.

3

Success Stories
of Ordinary,
Everyday People

I DON'T KNOW OF ANY OTHER WAY IN THE WORLD, SHORT OF HITTING A jackpot or winning a sweepstakes, that the average person can accumulate wealth and build financial security more easily than by investing in real estate.

When I said the average person, a friend of mine said, "You'd better not call anyone average because they're going to be turned off and won't be interested in what you have to say. No one wants to be told they're average. They all want to be considered unique." I guess I can answer that by saying my friend is partially right because I know each of us is unique in our own way. And those of us who've looked at real estate for profit and as an investment program are, as a group, very unique.

The truth, however, is that most of us are average. Very few of us ever become investment geniuses like the Donald Trumps of our society. The odds are pretty good that we'll never attain the position of a Lee Iacocca. I don't think that many of us, despite our dreams and fantasies, will become rich and famous. The chances of winning the sweepstakes or a lottery are very minimal at best for most of us. Also, as you and I both know, there aren't many among us who will inherit great sums of money.

That leaves most of us in the middle—just plain, average folks. We dress alike, drive the same kind of cars (with some variations), eat and travel alike, live in an average home with an average mortgage, have an average job and an average income, and a lot of us end up with an average retirement. The sad part is that retirement consists of the proverbial gold watch, an average pension, and a social security check that might or might not cover our needs.

Without financial security, our existence can be like living in a barren sandpit of life.

All this can and does happen to a million people every day of the week. It also can happen to you and me, unless we make plans to do something about it *now*.

When I tell this story to young people, they don't think it can happen to them. They more or less think, as I did and most of us did when we were younger, that they're immortal and probably will never grow old and need any security. It's something too remote and not worth thinking about—until it's too late.

The plain fact is, though, that no matter how hard we might fight it, we are all mortal and we're all going to grow old. If we want to grow old gracefully and in comfort, we better have some concern about security and the finances it takes to maintain that security. In fact, security is great and I recommend it, but we should want more than mere security. We should have a burning desire to have that security and go first class wherever we want to go.

THE TIME IS NOW TO BUILD FOR THE FUTURE

With the uncertainty of the future and the turmoil taking place with our social security system, we are left with a question we should all be asking ourselves: "What can I do to provide financial security and some sort of financial growth for my future?"

I don't think any of us want to be Joe Average, waiting for the monthly social security check and then wondering if there's enough money for a vacation or a trip—let alone going first class. I figure the smart person, the one who keeps his nose to the grindstone, the unique individual, will think long and hard about this fact. The smart person's going to want more than being in the social security line.

In a recent newspaper article, Lee Iacocca is quoted as saying, ". . . if you keep your nose to the grindstone and work at it, it's amazing how in a free society you can become as great as you want to be."

My experience has convinced me that anyone can escape from this average existence if they want, and that way is through real estate investment, which offers one of the very few opportunities for the average, common person to accumulate any sort of wealth and build financial security, a retirement program, and a way to experience the good things in life.

We might not reach the level of the very rich and famous, and it might not be as quick as the lottery drawing, but real estate, with its built-in financial components of:

- Rental income
- Contract for deed payments
- Cash in the bank

represents:

- Security
- Freedom from debt
- Independence
- First class accommodations

For any of us, *right now* is the best time to consider doing something about our future. I did. And if I, Joe Average, can do it, anyone can.

My life certainly was average. I was an average person living in an average neighborhood, raising an average family on an average income—until I discovered real estate. When I bought my first property I didn't have a lot of money, and that's certainly average. I had no special education beyond a college degree, and that's certainly no more than average. And believe me, I had no chance of any inheritance.

So, with the average income and average education, it was pretty clear that I wasn't going to make a lot of money as a brain surgeon, and I figured with my average background I wasn't going to make it big in the business world of pizza, fast-food, cookies, and computers. However, I did discover real estate—something I and anyone else, could do. Real estate was for me, Joe Average, a way to build financial wealth and security.

For some reason we seem to think that investment real estate is only for the wealthy land baron or the get-rich-quick television investors. Sometimes we're scared to death and think, ''I don't think I, Joe Average, have the ability, let alone the money, to invest in real estate.''

The truth is, though, that there are a lot of average people out there, just like you and me, who do own investment real estate and are doing very well with it. You probably don't read about them and you don't see them on television, but they're out there.

Don't expect to become an overnight millionaire. Take your time; buy one property at a time and build from there. Use common sense and you can change your average life into something more fulfilling. Real estate offers this fulfillment. It's an open-door business and is available to anyone. Believe me, anyone can do it.

Not only can anyone do it, but as far as I can see, for the average person, real estate is about the only business that offers many opportunities to the average person.

___

You don't have to be rich and important to succeed. Julius Caesar said, "I would rather be first in my village than second in Rome."

___

If you're not convinced yet, let's take a look at some of the average people's success stories in real estate.

JANE'S STORY OF SUCCESSFUL INVESTING

Jane, age 33, is a professional photographer. She has a good job, and an average income, is single, and lives in a large city. Since the time she left college, she has been renting an apartment or a duplex.

She told me once, "I paid my rent every month and found out that the $415 was going to my landlord, and he was buying this property using my money. I ended up with nothing but a receipt."

She came to me for some advice about investments and about her future. I recommended that she use her savings account for a down payment on a small duplex (Fig. 3-1). She could then live in one half, have the comfort of her own home and the security of never being evicted, and she could rent out the other half. With the income from the rental unit and her $415, she could easily make the payment on the mortgage, pay the taxes and insurance, and probably have enough left over to take care of the upkeep. Added to the investment was the ever-present income tax benefit of owning investment real estate.

Jane bought a duplex. It isn't the fanciest nor the newest, but it is within her financial range. It's totally adequate to fill her needs and is located in a stable neighborhood where her investment will remain secure.

The property she bought was an older, well-cared-for, two-bedroom duplex with a double garage. An elderly couple had lived in the property for over 40 years. The man died and his wife was moving into a nursing home.

Fig. 3-1. Low-priced, inexpensive duplexes like this can be the ideal starter for someone who wants to get away from renting and is willing to live in an older apartment until until he can afford something better. This property, if well maintained, will always hold its value and will, under good management, remain occupied. The starter investor—single, married, or whatever—can move in, get homestead rights, and start his real estate business with a comparatively small investment, and probably pay less than if renting. Once the mortgage is decreased, the equity can buy the next step up—a better duplex. (They call it upward mobility.)

After some negotiating, she was able to acquire a 10-year contract-for-deed* purchase for $59,000. The payment on this contract for deed is $674.29, which includes insurance but not taxes.

Rent on one-half the duplex brings $495 per month. She has moved into the other half and maintains homestead rights. With the $495 rent and the $415 she had been paying before, she's now able to save money.

She has investment property for her future; she is able to save money; and she has a two-bedroom apartment with a garage. Add one more benefit: she'll have the property paid for in full in about 15 years. In all probability, if she cares for the property, it'll increase in value during that 15-year period.

I asked her about the difficulties of managing the property, and she said, "There's nothing I can't handle. Oh sure, I've got to be concerned about getting good tenants, and taking care of the complaints and service calls, but for the time and effort I feel I'm being well paid. I've really got a little business of my own now."

This story is certainly an average story of an average person getting involved in real estate. Her next step can be to upgrade her living standard by establishing some equity in this property and buying another better duplex. She can keep the older one, plus the new one, and have a nice cash flow. I did tell her, however, that if she moves out of the one into another, she's going to lose the homestead rights and this could mean an additional $100 or more tax per month on the nonhomestead property.

Regardless, this story is a success story. It doesn't represent millions of dollars, but it's a start.

RON'S STORY OF REAL ESTATE

Ron is a middle-aged handyman. He's pretty sharp when it comes to fixing and repairing. He knows what he's doing and makes a good living at his occupation: being a jack of all trades and investing in real estate. You won't see Ron's story on television, but it's a beauty.

Ron has a few built-in benefits. He has no children, he is married, and his wife works full time as an office manager of a large corporation.

Ron and his wife have invested in various types of real estate over the years. If it wasn't for the tax write-off from the investment property, he and his wife would be in an extremely high income-tax bracket.

Ron's first investment was an older, run-down, single-family home. It was located in a nice middle-class neighborhood and had, when he bought it, great potential for growth in value through rejuvenation.

Figure 3-2 is an example of the kind of home with which he started.

---

*Contract for Deeds are discussed in depth in Chapter 7.

Fig. 3-2. For the brave, innovative, hard-working investor, a run-down, abandoned property in a well-kept, middle-class neighborhood can be a real profit maker. Remember, though, this type of rejuvenating takes a lot of work and time.

He doesn't own this home, but it gives you an idea of how money can be made through rejuvenation, what kinds of property to look for, and how you can acquire this type of property.

This home has an interesting story. I'd like to tell you about it.

This property had been abandoned some 15 years ago. The owner suffered a business failure, and didn't pay federal and state taxes, so the governments filed a *tax lien* against him, which covers all real estate. The liens and the mortgage amounted to more than the value of the property, so the owner walked away from it.

As a result, the bank foreclosed on the mortgage, and there were now federal and state tax liens, a bank mortgage that had accumulated 15 years of nonpayments, including interest, and 15 years of unpaid real estate taxes. This debt meant the property was virtually worthless.

To clear the title, the tax liens had to be satisfied, the bank mortgage had to be paid off, and the county taxes had to be brought up to date. In addition, the owner still had an interest. All this sounds like an impossible situation. It's not, and here's what happened.

The county officials were contacted and told that they'd be better off by getting this property cleared up and back on the tax rolls. The county attorney contacted the federal and state lien holders and convinced them that there was no way they could ever recover anything, that the property was deteriorating and they should do something to get it back as a viable property. The governments were convinced they wouldn't recover anything, so they agreed to release the tax liens. The county agreed to waive all the back taxes. The bank accepted a small payment to release the mortgage, and the owner gave a warranty deed for a minimal amount. All in all, this investor was able to acquire this property for $5,000.

The next step was to analyze whether it is worth investing the work, time, and money necessary to renovate and repair it and bring it up to value.

As you can see, the property is located in an excellent residential area. The basic structure is sound and in good condition. The building needs new siding, a new roof, some new windows, and a considerable amount of repair work on the inside. An eager, innovative, and hard-working individual can take a project like this and literally make thousands of dollars.

These types of foreclosed properties are available everywhere. It's a matter of getting the right price and knowing if there's sufficient potential to make a profit.

This fact is called to your attention because it's the kind of thing that Ron did. He turned the real estate business into a highly profitable venture.

Ron personally did all the remodeling and renovating of the properties he purchased. Most of the work was done on his off hours and weekends. His first project, this one-family house, netted him $9,500 profit.

His next project was something else. He bought an older, three-story, brick hotel. It was still operating marginally as a hotel; however, there were so many competitive motels that the small hotel business just wasn't very profitable.

Ron converted the rooms into small, one-bedroom apartments. Each unit had a kitchenette, bedroom, living room, and bathroom. Once the word was out that this conversion was taking place, there was an avalanche of requests for the apartments. They were filled almost as fast as he could convert them.

Ron was able to eliminate the costly management of a hotel operation, yet reap the good income of a smoothly run apartment business—with no vacancies.

He operated the business for several years with moderate success. Ron used the income to pay off the mortgage quickly, inasmuch as he didn't need to take anything out of the business for personal living expenses.

I don't know if he had it all paid off or not, but he did sell it on a contract for deed. I also don't know what the selling price was, but I know he made a bundle. Now he has a nice monthly check from the contract for deed. In fact, Joe Average could probably live quite comfortably on this check alone.

Over the years, Ron has continued to buy and sell fixer-uppers. Today, after about 15 years of investing, he's pretty well off. He owns rental property and some contract for deeds.

Ron is an average person who realized phenomenal success in the real estate business. He's a real life story, par excellence, of real estate investing.

Although he and I see one another regularly, the last thing in the world he needs is advice from me. As a matter of fact, there's a lot of Ron's information in this book.

SUSAN'S INVESTMENT PROGRAM

Susan is a 39-year-old single professional. Her income places her in the highest income tax bracket. She told me that she just got sick and tired of giving all her money to the government. She asked me, ''What can I do?''

My advice for her was to use the equity in her personal home as a down payment on a nice, well-maintained duplex—something that wouldn't take a lot of management. I told her to look for something that would come close to cash flow. She needed enough rental income to pay the expenses.

I did tell her that, even if she didn't have enough rental income and had to use her own money, a duplex was the best place in the world to invest this money. For one thing, it was sure a lot better than giving it to the government. Most important to her was the fact that all the real estate losses, if there were any, could be reported on her personal income. This constituted the great tax break she needed.

She found an excellent duplex. The property wasn't available on a contract-for-deed purchase, but she had an excellent credit rating, good equity in her personal home, and some cash reserve. The equity from her home was enough for the down payment and closing costs.

Figure 3-3 is an exceptional investment property. It's in excellent condition; surrounding properties are also in A-1 condition. The property has no deteriorating factors. It's very rentable and has a good financial picture.

The income from this property is $10,800 per year. The expenses are minimal because the property is in such good condition. Real estate taxes are $2,200 and insurance is $395 per year. There are no maintenance costs and no advertising because there aren't vacancies.

After expenses, there's a net gross profit of $8,110.95 per year,

Fig. 3-3. Here's a property for an investor who can't take the time to take care of properties. This proper-ty is very rentable, has good income, involves no work, and can lead to future investments once the equity is established.

or $675 per month. This property could support a 9 percent, 25-year mortgage at a purchase price of $80,000.

The property is valued at $105,000. Without a down payment, the payment on this property would be $869. That means the investor has to have a down payment to buy the property. The alternatives are to make larger payments with personal income or buy the property with the payment of $675 per month and a balloon payment at the end of the contract. Keep in mind there's also the tax write-off on the property. This write-off carries over to personal income, which certainly is an added income factor.

After managing and caring for this property for a few years, Susan found out it didn't interfere at all with her business career. She decided, after seeing her investment grow and the income tax savings, that it was time to buy more properties.

Since this initial investment she's bought a three-plex, which again is in good condition and doesn't take a lot of management (Fig. 3-4). This average person has ended up with a great tax write-off and a substantial equity. I predict someday she'll be a real-estate millionaire.

MARK'S REAL ESTATE INVESTMENT

Mark worked for the government as a foreign service officer for 25 years. As a result of starting early (just out of college), he was a young man

Fig. 3-4. This property is the next step up for the "passive" investor. It is an excellent three-plex, produces excellent income, and is very rentable. It's the kind of property that will, with time, develop into a real equity builder because it will never decrease in value.

when he retired. He figured he could easily start another career. At first he looked at various jobs, but all of them meant working from 9 to 5, a boss to answer to, and no freedom to come and go as he pleased.

During the time he worked for the government, he had a good income. Most of his expenses were paid so he was able to establish a good savings account.

After I visited with him and we talked about real estate investment and its advantages, he decided to take some of his savings and buy some property.

He has since told me this is one of the best moves he could have made. He started a second career, which developed into a full-time business, giving him the freedom he wished and an excellent income. He could work when he wanted and vacation as he pleased.

When he did work, he spent most of his time remodeling and rejuvenating apartments. This work substantially increased the value of the property without increasing his costs much because he was able to do a lot of it himself. In addition, as he improved each apartment, he could, and did, raise the rents. So he experienced the appreciation in value of his property and an increase in rents—just like a proverbial money machine.

He told me once, "Those rent checks the tenants bring in each month have paid off my mortgages. Now there's enough money that I draw a pretty good salary out of the business. I'd be willing to bet," he said, "I make about $500 an hour for the time I spend managing and taking care of the property."

JIM AND MARY'S INVESTMENTS

When Jim and Mary got married, they bought a nice town house in the city. They both worked at regular jobs and both earned good income. About four years ago, their tax accountant told them they should find a way to protect their income because they were paying too much income tax.

They came to me and asked my advice. I knew Jim was a general construction worker, and my thought was he could handle a small investment property—something that needed some rejuvenation. I figured he could easily do this kind of work on the weekends and have a good investment.

We started looking into various properties in their neighborhood and found a good starter. With very little work, the property could easily be appreciated. It was located in a good neighborhood so it constituted a sound investment.

Jim and Mary were in a high income tax bracket. They were concerned that some day they might lose the tax write-off under the new law, which says that owners of rental property with adjusted incomes of $100,000 or less can take up to $25,000 in losses per year against their regular income. I assured them there would be no great concern because I think the law will change.

As a matter of fact, the government has discovered there are a growing number of real estate foreclosures because the property owner with an income over $125,000 can't write off the losses. The legislature is pressing hard for new legislation that would allow owners of rental properties to deduct losses incurred by the properties. The deductions could be used to offset income earned from salaries and other income sources.

Although this couple has just started investing, they've found it to be just what they're looking for: a tax write-off as well as a savings. In the short time they've been in business, they've realized a $15,000 increase in value through renovating the property. This savings will grow with each property. If they stick with it they won't be average—that is, financially speaking.

A BUSINESSMAN INVESTS IN REAL ESTATE

Duane is a 41-year-old, self-employed, successful, small business operator living in a rural community. He and his wife have teenage children. They've owned their home for a number of years. Everything Duane has he acquired on his own through hard work—no inheritance and no gifts.

When he was 29 years of age, Duane started buying small fixer-upper

Fig. 3-5. This is an example of an older, large, three-story home converted into a six-plex. This kind of property can be made into excellent smaller rental units. Older homes like this usually have exquisite ornate woodwork and some stained glass windows, and so are attractive to certain people. Most of these old mansions were built as solid as the Rock of Gibralter and, with good care, should stand for years. Multiunits like these are good profit-makers.

investment properties. He and his wife spent long hours after business upgrading the properties.

His first investment turned out to be a good buy, but was more of a learning experience than a profit maker. Duane's next property was a six-plex. Well, what it was was a large old home converted into three stories of apartments, two on each level (Fig. 3-5). Rental income is good from this kind of property, especially when considering the investment made.

In this type building you're not competing with any other market, either the low-rent housing or the middle-class apartments. Most apartments in older converted homes consist of one-bedroom apartments suited for the single working person.

They usually can be purchased at a price the average investor can afford. This purchase price usually is determined by the rental income. If the rental income is sufficient to make the mortgage payment and cover the overhead, the purchase price is right.

Invariably rental income increases. I've been in the business for 25 years and never once during that time have I had to lower rents. Just the opposite is true: every year the rents have increased. The nice thing about this, and especially for the six-plex purchased by Duane, is that the basic cost of the property remains the same.

Since purchasing the six-plex, Duane and his family have continued buying properties. Today his real estate holdings are worth a lot more than his well-managed and successful small business. Someday I predict he and his family will live on easy street from the investment properties. And, I don't mean he's going to have to wait until he's 65 years old.

The last I heard, he owns a six-plex, several four-plexes, and several single-family homes. And, his investments are growing yearly.

As we visited and talked about real estate, I asked him, "Why did you decide to buy investment property? After all, you were doing pretty well in the business world?" He answered, with great pride, "Back some years ago I read a few real estate books that got me thinking. I figured I could do it and thought if I wanted to accumulate and establish any sort of wealth this is a way it can be done. Sure, I was earning a good living, although everything I made was spent and gone at the end of each month. First there was some reluctance on my part buying that first piece of property. It was really tough making the decision because it meant more debt and more payments. But as I look back, I can tell you it was one of the smartest things I've done.

There's more to Duane's story. He said, "Over the past 12 years I've gained some great experience and learned a lot about the real estate business. I've accumulated about $260,000 in real estate equity. That's money I'd never have had if it wasn't for my investing in real estate. It's not all a bed of roses, though, because there are tenant complaints, vacancies to fill, backed-up sewers, and dirty refrigerators to clean. All these things need constant attention, but between my wife and now my kids who are in school, we can handle the properties and management pretty well. It's nice because all these things can be done on our time.''

Duane is an average person with an average success story in real estate. He hasn't made a million, but he's certainly doing very well.

A PLUMBER GETS INVOLVED IN REAL ESTATE

Paul is a 42-year-old plumber. He's worked hard, made a good living, but discovered he wasn't really making any financial progress. His income increased every year, but so did his expenses and standard of living.

Paul told me when he bought his first property, "I was fixing other people's plumbing and it seemed to me that if those people were making money in real estate I should get into it myself. I also thought if I've got to fix people's plumbing I might as well be fixing my own."

Since then Paul has bought various smaller units of investment property. He said, "My wife and I take care of the apartments. We really don't work that hard on it and don't put in that many hours. I do know I'm making more money in real estate with the equity I'm earning than I make as a plumber."

I have a feeling Paul doesn't need any advice from me and I predict that if he continues and doesn't burn himself out with overwork at his occupation and the real estate business, he'll have a nice nest egg some day.

A CONSTRUCTION SUPERINTENDENT BUYS REAL ESTATE

Jim is 53 years old. Over the years he's bought a lot of properties, specializing mainly in fixer-uppers. I suppose that he has an accumulation of 30 to 35 rental units.

He told me once that all of this was done on a part-time basis, and that he was easily able to invest and fix up real estate without it interfering with his business.

In the very near future he's talking about retiring from his job and taking care of his apartments. He's accumulated equity over the years; his mortgages are paid off so the rent income is clear for him to be able to draw a pretty good salary.

Jim's no more than an average, everyday person, working at an average job, who found real estate to his liking. Today I'd be willing to bet Jim's net worth is near $1 million, and that's money he'd never have had if it wasn't for his real estate investing. The average person at an average job with an average (or even above average) income just can't save that much money in a lifetime.

All these stories are about simple, common, ordinary folks like you meet and talk to everyday. Every community is loaded with them. I've talked to a lot of them, and have yet to find a successful real estate investor who hasn't been totally sold on the idea. It just goes to show you it takes no special talent, no training other than learning some of the basics of real estate, and not a great deal of money to get started. Anyone can do it.

4

How to Avoid
the Pitfalls of
Real Estate Investing

IT WOULD BE FOOLISH FOR ME TO TELL YOU THERE AREN'T FAILURES AND setbacks, financial losses and, yes, even bankruptcies in the real estate business. Many investors make bad decisions about managing their properties; some don't watch their finances, and some make bad investments that can eventually lead to financial setbacks and even total failures. This chapter, along with Chapter 11, Managing Real Estate Through a Crisis, is meant to show you what to look for and how to avoid failure.

So you won't be misled and think that the real estate business and every investment property is a bed of roses, I think it's important to let you know about some of the mistakes, bad investments, and problems related to investment property. The best way to do so is to tell you some of the real life experiences of investors. The individuals in these stories will remain nameless, for obvious reasons, but their experiences are real and can relate what happens when there's a lack of good old common sense in owning and managing real estate.

Let's take a look.

OVERRENOVATING CAUSES FINANCIAL FAILURE

This is the story of a 49-year-old general construction contractor. You'd think a general contractor would have enough knowledge about real estate so that he wouldn't fail. But that's not the case.

As I wrote this story I found what I perceived to be a flaw in the character of this person. He was a know-it-all; he thought he was just a little better than everyone else, and his arrogance was overbearing. He never requested anyone's advice and went into things entirely on his own.

For the first 10 years in business as a contractor, he did well building and selling houses. However, then he got the idea he could invest in real estate on his own. He bought some older apartment buildings that needed overhauling. As he did this work, he put in the best of everything. Rather than installing inexpensive cupboards, bathrooms, air conditioners, and other improvements, he bought the best and most expensive. What happened was that he ended up with a new "old" apartment building. With the original purchase price of the building and the cost of renovation, he could easily have bought a new apartment complex. Now he ended up with an old building and had to charge the same rents as if it was new in order to recover his costs. He did this with several properties and ultimately went into debt to a point of no return.

Of course I could not advise this investor, nor would he have taken my advice in the first place. However, I can tell you the mistakes he made and show you how to avoid them.

First, if you buy older property that needs renovating, don't overrenovate. For example, find inexpensive metal kitchen cupboards, rather than expensive wood cupboards. Buy quality, but inexpensive carpeting. When it comes to carpeting an apartment, the color isn't all that important, but price is. Shop around and get the best deal for carpeting, as well as all the materials you use.

Second, watch the costs so you don't overspend and eventually lose the property by putting too much money into it.

Third, contact other investors before you take on this kind of project. Get other opinions and advice. Also question carpenters, lumberyard managers, and others who've had experience with real estate.

BURNOUT CAN COST PROFITS

Let's look at a government employee, who has an average job, average life-style, and average, middle-class home. He did have a better than average mind, and with this mind discovered he could do better for himself and start a good investment program in real estate.

For 15 years he bought and sold fixer-upper properties, doing the work on his vacations, on weekends, and whenever he could find time. He did all right for a number of years. However, he overdid it, and burned himself out. He didn't take the needed vacations, was gone from his home and family on weekends and nights, and pretty soon had more than he could handle while still working a full-time job.

He came to me for advice as things began looking rather bleak. He confided in me that he was getting tired of working at the property, had accumulated all this real estate, and now didn't know what to do. He also told me he was devoted to his church and spent a lot of time and money in the church.

I first told him I thought he was giving too much, both to the church and to his real estate business. I suggested to him that he either consider selling the property or hire management. I told him that if he didn't, the property would deteriorate quickly. The fact is, by the time he got to me it was almost too late.

Deterioration only takes a short time. I noticed as he became more discontent with the tenant problems, fixing this and fixing that, handling complaints, and filling vacancies, he began to let things go. At first he lost some good tenants and then couldn't get good tenants to replace those he lost. He ended up with some slow-paying and no-paying tenants, which only added to his dilemma. What he got into was what I call a real estate sinkhole.

After a couple of years of this deterioration, he finally sold the property. He was only able to get market value because the properties needed some rejuvenation, which he didn't care to do. As a result, he lost the appreciation he had gained over the years. However, he did end up in pretty good condition because he was able to recover all the equity he'd built, so it wasn't a total disaster.

The point of the story is that anyone in the business must realize his limitations. It's like any other business: you can't overdo it.

Despite this sad story of real estate, I still believe the rewards far outweigh the liabilities and trouble. It certainly beats anything else and any other business I know.

ABSENTEE OWNERSHIP LEADS TO PROBLEMS

Here's the story of an individual who bought an older four-plex in a city located 100 miles from where he lived. He didn't come to me and seek advice before he bought the property. Probably he knew what the answer would be. I'd have told him right out that absentee ownership is dangerous and not a good investment program. Nevertheless, he bought a property with the expectation of being able to manage it from his home 100 miles away.

The first mistake he made was renting with no control over the tenants. He had no idea how they paid their bills, and this started him on the first of a series of problems.

Next, driving 100 miles to handle complaints and fix plumbing turned out to be very expensive and time consuming. Ultimately he had to hire someone to make all the repairs. This led to the next problem: being at the mercy of the service people. He had to pay whatever they charged. He was unable to do any bargain shopping. When a sewer was backed up, it had to be cleaned out right away.

To make this story short, the property turned sour for this investor. He lost the property on a mortgage foreclosure, and now he's back on the beat as a police officer working for his pension.

PERSONAL OVERSPENDING ENDS IN DISASTER

Let's look at a couple who started investing at a fairly early age and right from scratch. Their first property was mortgaged for almost its full value. However, as a couple, they were a good team and right from the start their business was successful. They gave excellent service to their tenants and had good, clean apartments so they never had a loss due to vacancies. In fact, usually there was a waiting line for their apartments.

They continued their operation for a number of years, bought more properties, increased their values, and continued the good service. The cash flow was tremendous, but so were the expenses and mortgage payments.

They started living a high life-style. They began dipping into the monthly rent checks to cover personal expenses. First there was a new car, then new household furniture, a plush summer home, and then exotic vacations. This uncontrolled spending went on for about a year and then the problems set in. From that point on it was down hill. First, there wasn't money to pay the taxes. Upkeep and maintenance were ignored and then payments on the property weren't made.

A wise old philosopher once said, "If you love money better than higher values, may you make a million dollars and spend it all on doctors."

Ultimately they lost the properties, all of their investment, and this excellent business they built up. In addition, the experience was so stressful that the husband lost his health.

Is there an answer to such a pathetic story? Sure there is. You must realize you can't live beyond your means. You must constantly be alert to the financial affairs of the business and not let things get out of hand.

Many similar stories exist, but you get the idea. Enough said on this subject because we want to get on to more positive investment programs.

5

The Fixer-Upper: The Smart Way to Real Estate Profits

THERE'S NO DOUBT IN MY MIND THAT ONE OF THE BEST POTENTIAL PROFit makers in real estate is the fixer-upper, especially for the ambitious beginning investor.

Rejuvenation is a money-maker and has many financial rewards for a number of reasons.

Property can be purchased at a reasonably inexpensive price if it's in need of rejuvenation. As a result, there's great potential for financial growth as the property is improved. The property will, in fact, increase in value with each and every improvement that's made, right from the start of general cleanup to general repair and including a paint job.

Usually, with good planning and competent rejuvenation management (which simply means watching the expenses), for every dollar invested of time and money, there's at least a twofold return and many times much more. There's no proof of this, but it's just one of those things that happens with real estate.

Rejuvenation is an ongoing process. As the improvements are made, modest rent increases can follow. Hence, the increase in rent eventually will pay for the improvements. Once the improvements are paid for, the next step is to invest the profit back into more rejuvenation, which will increase the value of the property. This increase in value justifies increasing the rents. It's almost a perpetual money machine.

Every penny spent on rejuvenating the property is tax deductible. Not only is the expense deductible and charged against the property, but any losses can be carried over to the investor's personal income.

So as the property increases in value, the investor is depreciating all the costs.

Last, but not least, with each improvement there's an increase in value, which represents equity, and equity means borrowing power. For instance, let's say the property is purchased for $50,000 and the rejuvenating costs are $5,000. In all probability that rejuvenation will increase the property value probably to $65,000. That increase means there's $10,000 net profit or equity and there's nothing involved but the $5,000 plus time and work.

I did this. I bought a run-down six-plex for $60,000 (not in New York or San Francisco). Over a period of 5 years, I rejuvenated the property—nothing major. I upgraded some of the kitchens and bathrooms, replaced some worn-out carpeting, installed electric heat, replaced an old steam boiler, and did some cleaning and general repair. When the work was completed, the building was appraised at $110,000.

In any rejuvenation, all the equity can be used as borrowing power to buy more real estate.

BENEFITS OF REJUVENATING PROPERTY

Obviously the financial gains, which are indisputable, are great. However, there are other benefits in investing in these kinds of properties, especially when you consider prices of the traditional A-1 investment property (and there's certainly nothing wrong with buying A-1 investment property). With the A-1 properties there's not as much to gain. Of course, there's not as much work involved either because the A-1 is usually in excellent rentable condition and doesn't take the work and time the rejuvenated property does.

Another benefit of rejuvenation is that the investor has complete control over the location, the neighborhood, and the property. It's simply a matter of waiting until something comes along that's appealing and that has good potential. Remember, there's nothing that says you must buy the first property that comes along.

Keep in mind when looking for investment properties to avoid slums, pick a stable, growing community, and don't invest in locations that have deteriorating circumstances, i.e., near freeways, close to industrial developments, and deteriorating neighborhoods.

Sweat equity—the work, energy, and effort put into the property—pays off many fold. Look at what can be done without investing any dollars: clean yard, trim trees and shrubs, eliminate debris and junk, make repairs, clean halls, basement, stairways, and premises.

Small things like this that don't cost anything will not increase the property by thousands of dollars. However, the improvement of the property can and will make a great difference as to what kind of tenants the property attracts. The better the tenant, the more valuable the property.

All rejuvenation work can be done by anyone. It's not necessary to be a talented plumber, carpenter, or electrician. It helps to be a "jack of all trades," and later in the book I'll discuss some of these jobs that can be done.

REJUVENATION INCREASES RENTABILITY

As I've said before, there's no doubt that a few simple projects can make a difference. For instance, a potential tenant who sees a cluttered yard, a junk-filled basement or dirt throughout the hallways, entry, and property, and worn-out carpeting is going to be turned off. Caring for these simple tasks will attract a better class tenant and better class tenants are money-makers.

If you're willing to take the time, devote some effort and work, and get involved, there's money to be made out there in the rejuvenation of real estate.

Incidentally, there's one added feature with rejuvenating property. Once the job is done and you can stand back and see an improved property, it can give you a feeling of accomplishment. It's a job well done. There's pride in ownership.

HOW TO FIND A FIXER-UPPER

First of all, a *fixer-upper* isn't a slum, an abandoned or dilapidated property, or a shelled-out building. A fixer-upper is an occupied property that has been neglected by the owner. In general, it's a property that needs to be upgraded and repaired at a minimum cost. Most of the time such a property has been neglected by the owner for one of the following reasons:

- The property has been depreciated fully and there's no longer a tax write-off.
- The owner has paid off the mortgage, has no intention of putting more money back into the property, and just wants to sell it.
- The owner doesn't want to take the time or effort to fix things up. The property has probably produced income, established equity, and appreciated. In the eyes of the owner it's time to get out.
- The property is managed for an absentee owner.

Finding this kind of property certainly isn't all that difficult. Following is a list of potential sellers and sources of information:

- Other apartment owners and investors
- Apartment owners association
- Building-supply firms and carpenters
- Newspaper advertisements
- Lawn signs
- Real estate agents

Ask! Most of the properties will be owned by other investors. Don't depend totally on real estate agents because a lot of sellers don't list their properties. Buying direct can be a money-saver because there's no agent's fee to pay.

NEGOTIATE THE TERMS

As I've said before, there's not much competition out there because a lot of buyers don't want to take the time and effort required to operate an investment property. If you want to take on these projects you're in the driver's seat when you are making deals.

Therefore, as you're entering into a purchase, negotiate the terms of purchase to fit your program. You can usually tell the seller how much you can afford for a down payment, what interest you can pay, and how much you can afford to pay on the contract for deed. (Most investment properties are sold on a contract for deed.)

As you negotiate, use every negative aspect of the property. Point out all the defects and let the seller know it's going to cost money to get that property back in A-1, serviceable condition.

Check closely on the financial status of the property. Ask to see the precise records. If the property is losing money, let the seller know. Point it out to him so he knows you know.

Whatever you do, don't, under any circumstances, take the word of the real estate agent about the finances of the property. The agent is going to tell you everything is profitable and doing well. In fact, he'll tell you anything to make the sale.

Also check the vacancies. All investors have a precise record of how their properties are doing, showing the tenants, rental income, and vacancies. The number of vacancies can tell a lot. If they're high there's something wrong with the property.

Ask to see the exact records and then use those records to negotiate.

WHAT TO LOOK FOR IN A FIXER-UPPER

The number one clue to a good buy in the fixer-upper is a property that needs to be painted. A bad paint job is one of the most significant depreciating factors of real estate.

Fig. 5-1. This is a fairly attractive house, but you can see how the looks are deteriorated because it needs to be painted. You can almost visualize the potential for increasing the value with only a simple paint job. As an owner, if you're ready to sell, don't overlook painting first. A few hundred dollars can convert into a thousand or more in appreciation.

Take a look at Fig. 5-1. It's not difficult to realize what a coat of paint can do to increase the value of this property.

Another factor that affects the looks, as well as the value of property, is a general unkept look. Cluttered property, junk in the yard, weeds and sucker trees growing around the foundation, an unmowed lawn, and trees that need trimming all detract from properties.

Following is a list of other things to look for when shopping for an investment property, such as:

- Interior housekeeping
- Entryways and halls that need to be painted
- Worn-out carpeting
- Run-down kitchens and bathrooms

On the exterior of the premises, check:

- General condition of exterior, paint, damaged siding
- Condition of roof
- Grounds, lawns, and trees
- Walks and driveways
- Exterior lighting
- Garage
- Doors and windows

Also check the basement. A basement that's strewn with junk and clutter left over from previous tenants is not only unattractive, but contributes to deterioration. Figure 5-2 is the kind of thing I'm talking about.

Most of all, look for low-priced properties in high-priced neighborhoods. Any rejuvenation pays off handsomely with this kind of property because the surroundings will contribute to the appreciation.

Fig. 5-2. As an owner, you should keep premises, basements, and hallways clean and neat.

THE COST AND TIME INVOLVED

Don't get involved with major renovation if you're not ready. This fact is especially true for the beginning investor.

Fixer-uppers mean just that—they must be fixed up. Avoid projects in which the work is time-consuming and costly, such as:

- Electrical, plumbing, heating, and air conditioning
- New roof
- New siding
- Disintegrated basement
- Sagging floors and ceiling
- Structurally unsound foundation
- Slum properties

It's a good idea to prepare a checklist of the things to look for when you are analyzing a potential fixer-upper. It can mean a lot of savings in time and effort.

Fig. 5-3. This kind of property has great potential if it's reasonably priced, is in a fairly stable neighborhood, and is in good enough condition that revitalization will work.

Now, let's take a look at some properties so you have an idea of what to look for in a good investment property. Figure 5-3 is a prime example of a property that needs rejuvenation and makes a good beginning investment. Most of the work that's needed on this property can be done in time; that is, there's nothing urgently in need of repair.

As you can see, the building needs to be painted. That alone can make a tremendous difference.

This property is a four-plex that provides adequate income to cover the costs of operation and the price of the property. Following are the income and expense figures. They can differ from community to community and neighborhood to neighborhood.

The total income from this property is $10,080 rent, plus $300 per year washer and dryer income. Expenses are as follows:

Fuel (heat is furnished in apartments)	$1,580
Utilities for lights in basement and hallways	668
Repair and maintenance	600
Advertising for vacancies (low vacancy factor)	12
Insurance	315
Real estate tax	1,490
Soft water service (now charged back to tenants)	29

When the math is completed we have a balance of $5,686, or $473.80 per month *net gross profit*, which means the profit before any interest and principal is paid. If the property can be purchased for $57,000 on a 25-year contract at 9 percent interest, the payment will be $471.95 per month, which means it would produce cash flow.

Figure 5-4 shows a property in the process of being rejuvenated. It represents a good beginner investment. This kind of run-down property usually can be bought at a discounted price. It's a one-family property so there's not a lot of space with which to become involved, but the potential for profit is still there.

This property is the kind of property that takes some time, effort, and a little bit of money, but I think an investor can realize a good profit on this kind of venture.

The property shown in Fig. 5-5 could be considered a marginal investment for the beginning rejuvenation investor. It depends entirely on how much time, effort, work, and money can be put into the property.

As you can see, it's run down. The eaves around the house are rotted and need to be replaced. Some of the siding is in need of repair. A lot of this work could be considered heavy duty and could be more than the investor could handle.

Fig. 5-4. Here's a smaller, one-family, run-down house that's in the process of being rejuvenated. The old porch has been torn off, which is sometimes very advisable. Shabby, dilapidated porches don't add much to an investment property. They're expensive to maintain and don't bring in any income. Think of this property as an investment if you have the time, energy, and know-how to fix and repair.

There's great potential for the property, however. The financial picture indicates that it could make some money if it were managed properly. It's an older family home converted into three rental units. The age, quaintness, hardwood floors, and atmosphere of the building have attracted college faculty as tenants. Thus, there has been dependable occupancy. The rents are $6,480 per year.

The expenses on the building run a little high. For instance, the owner pays the heat and part of the utilities. This expense comes to $1,082 for heat and $684 for hall and basement lights. Some of the expenses could be cut down if the utilities and heat were watched more carefully. Repairs cost $463; insurance, $423; and real estate tax, $1,262.

After expenses are deducted there is a net gross income of $2,566. Add to that income laundry equipment income of $210 per year. With the net profit, this property could support a $28,000, 9 percent, 25-year

Fig. 5-5. Properties like this can usually keep rents down and occupancy up if you keep them attractive and do not let them slide into a slum.

mortgage. (Incidentally, these figures are before depreciation tax allowance is considered.)

The point is that this property does have potential. It's the kind of property that a rejuvenation investor must look at closely before becoming involved in it. Some of the work might turn out to be too expensive; on the other hand, if the investor has the capability and can do the work on his own, it lessens the costs, obviously.

REJUVENATE, RENOVATE, OR REJECT

Some properties just don't make sense for the beginning investor. A major overhaul on a property can be costly and time-consuming. Getting too involved can be a loser. It can be not only a loser as far as money and time are concerned, but an investor can lose his interest in investing if

Fig. 5-6. Some properties should be avoided by nonexperienced investors. Properties like this can be so overwhelming that a new person in the rejuvenation business can be turned off before starting. Know how to determine the rejuvenator and the reject. Those things beyond rejuvenation take lots of time, skilled labor, and money. Don't get involved with property that'll break you both emotionally and financially.

he takes on more than he can handle and burns out.

The kind of property you see in Fig. 5-6 takes some major overhauling. It's best for the beginning investor to reject this kind of investment.

While on the subject of burn-out, it's important to know your limitations, both as far as work concerned and money invested. When looking for investments, analyze the project before making a final commitment. Set your goals and know what you can do.

Have a general idea of what repairs will cost. Ask advice from others. Take a carpenter or lumberyard manager to the property and get his help. If you have friends in the real estate business, either investors or agents, ask for their advice and help.

REJUVENATION PROJECTS FOR AMATEURS

Paint. As you know, painting is comparatively inexpensive, especially if you do the work yourself or with family members. Painting can be done on weekends and vacations. A fresh new paint job is easy and inexpensive, can be done by anyone, and increases the value of property.

Clean Up. The yard and premises can be rejuvenated with no cost. Simple inexpensive tasks like getting grass to grow, eliminating weeds and sucker trees, and starting some inexpensive shrubbery can add tremendously to the appearance and value of a property.

Interior Clean Up. Housekeeping is important to rental property. Clean, well-lighted hallways, basements, and storage rooms are not hard to maintain. I know some managers, including myself, who let things go for a period of time and pretty soon it's a mess. We seem to get accustomed to looking at that cluttered mess and do nothing about it. It's carelessness and isn't a part of the good housekeeping manual of real estate investing.

Refuse. Garbage-collection areas and garbage cans can give a bad impression and diminish the overall appearance of a property. Keeping the area clean, neat, and in good shape is not expensive, nor is the cost of a new garbage can.

Front Entry and Doors. The first impression a potential tenant gets of a property is the front entry. Make sure it's clean, well kept, and well lighted. Paint, if necessary, to make entry more attractive.

Have a clean and adequate mail box for each tenant.

Rejuvenate a Basement. Basements become a collect-all in apartment buildings. Tenants come and go and leave a variety of items. Eventually this accumulation must be cleaned out. A clean basement improves the looks and attractiveness of a building, especially to potential tenants.

Basements can be converted into profit-makers. If there's sufficient space, you can have private storage lockers for tenants. They can be built inexpensively and they add value to the property.

Install laundry equipment if it isn't already there. Tenants like having this service on the premises so they don't need to go to a Laundromat. Used laundry equipment can be purchased, rebuilt and in good condition, from commercial services. Charge whatever the going rate is and it becomes a profit-maker.

Always keep the furnace area in a basement clean and in good condition, not only for appearance, but for fire prevention.

Inside Apartment Clean Up. A dirty, grimey kitchen and bathroom can be a real turnoff to a potential tenant. It takes very little effort and time, and practically no money to keep these areas in good order. Check these areas:

- Kitchen cupboards
- Corners

- Sinks, tub, and stool
- Dirty toilet seat
- Floors
- Stove and refrigerator
- Carpet

Rejuvenating a kitchen can be inexpensive, but really adds to the attractiveness and rentability. Consider replacing older wooden kitchen cupboards with metal cupboards, a new metal sink basin, and a stainless steel sink. These inexpensive touches add tremendously to the attractiveness of an apartment. These touches alone can be a factor in charging more rent.

Everyone likes to have a nice, clean, and bright kitchen. Make sure the kitchen, above all else, is clean.

The bathroom is another room that can be inexpensively upgraded. A new toilet seat can make a world of difference. Replacing an old dirty medicine chest is an inexpensive addition. The bathroom, like the kitchen, should be kept clean.

Locks and Security. People like to have a secure place to live. Keep good working locks on the doors and windows. Incidentally, it's a good idea to keep one apartment key. Periodically tenants will call and say they've locked their key inside the apartment.

Insulation and Energy-saving Devices. Simple things, like stripping doors and windows against air leaks, are inexpensive. Most weather stripping can be installed by a novice. You can rent a blower to add attic insulation.

Perpetual Rejuvenation. It's a good idea to upgrade apartments and properties on an ongoing basis. Don't let things slide; pretty soon they can become overwhelming and out of control. Set aside time to check the properties and do the work that needs to be done at the time.

Advanced Rejuvenation and Renovation. Some projects take more time, effort, and money. Advanced rejuvenation can mean converting larger older homes into multiunit apartments or converting large oversized apartments into smaller, more compatible, and rentable apartments.

I'd recommend that you not take on renovation work until you know the business, have the capital to invest, and learn some carpentry and repair skills. This work is not rejuvenation because it entails tearing out walls, remodeling rooms, replacing entire kitchens and bathrooms, and remodeling the exterior of buildings. It's a part of advanced real estate investing and is an entire book within itself.

6

How to Get
Real Estate Financing

REMEMBER, I SAID THAT BUYING THE FIRST PIECE OF INVESTMENT PROPerty isn't all that easy? Well, getting financing for that first investment isn't easy either.

Most investors I know, including myself, started in the business on a literal shoestring. Having no money to start meant it took some searching to get financing. For instance, I had to borrow against my personal home in order to get started.

Common sense tells us that it takes money to buy real estate—or anything else for that matter. There's no such thing as something for nothing.

IS IT SAFE TO USE HOME EQUITY
OR INSURANCE CASH VALUE FOR FINANCING?

At the time I financed my home to buy investment property, my first thought was that I might be jeopardizing the roof over my head. However, the way it worked out, it was one of the best moves I've ever made. It's something I've never regretted for one minute, and since that time I've used this equity for many investments.

I'm convinced that, if you see a good property, if you're ready to make the move, if you can get financing with your home equity without paying high interest and points, there's no reason not to use it for investments.

For some reason we've developed a security blanket that we hate to give up when our home is paid off. I suppose it's part of the Great

American Dream. In my mind, though, it really doesn't represent that much. For one thing, you can't use that equity unless you borrow against it. There's no way to spend it and it really doesn't mean that much. I'd rather have a large loan on my home with several investment properties, than have my home paid off and no investments.

Another source of financing is life insurance cash value, which incidentally has a much lower rate of interest than a conventional bank loan.

I have a friend who borrowed on his life insurance and was able to get enough money to make a down payment on a nice four-plex. The good thing about this loan was that there wasn't any set plan for payments. In this way, he was able to get the property going well and, once it started making a profit, he paid off the life insurance company.

If there's some hesitancy on your part about using this life insurance cash value for loans, do the following. Buy another insurance policy to cover that loan. This new insurance policy can be a tax deduction as part of the cost of the real estate.

After you watch some of the television investment programs, you can easily be led to believe that getting financing for investment property is easy. But I can tell you, no matter how many of these get-rich-quick schemes you see, there's no such thing as easy financing and easy money for real estate investment property. As a matter of fact, I don't think anyone should give you the impression that buying real estate and financing it is an easy-come, easy-go proposition. I make this statement because, in my experience, obtaining financing is an integral, serious, and important part of the real estate investment business that should be fully understood.

I know that if you don't take this important part of the real estate business seriously, you can become easily discouraged. I've seen more people disheartened about buying real estate because they thought it was a matter of walking into the bank, getting the money, and closing the deal the same day. It just doesn't work that way, though.

On the other hand, there isn't any reason to discourage anyone from seeking financing and buying real estate, despite the inconveniences, which I'll point out as I go on. There's money out there; it's just a matter of finding the best deal and the best source.

IT COSTS MONEY TO BUY INVESTMENT PROPERTY

I wish I could tell you that I've found a plan where you could buy all the property you wanted with no money down and no closing costs. However, that isn't the real world of real estate.

Most bankers and sellers expect money to change hands—from the buyer's hands to the seller's. Part of this exchange comes in the form of a down payment; another part is closing costs.

Sometimes the amount of money it takes to complete a deal can vary. A good financial status, good credit rating, some equity in your home, life insurance cash value, bonds, stocks, or other assets—all these things will help in negotiating with the banker and the seller. It only makes sense that lenders are going to be more willing to take a chance on somebody who has built up a good record. A good credit rating will provide one of the best financing vehicles for a contract for deed purchase that you can find.

Let's talk more about financing negotiations. Our negotiating skills can be honed well and get us into the real estate business once we've established the basic ingredients: credit, equity, and reputation.

Regardless of how much we want to negotiate ourselves into nothing-down real estate purchases, there's money involved that must be paid. As far as I can see, most of the following costs are paid by the buyer:

- Attorney fees for title opinion
- Deed preparation
- Appraisal fee
- Title search
- Title registration
- Mortgage tax
- Credit report
- Down payment

NOTHING-DOWN INVESTMENT PURCHASES

We've been bombarded on television and in some books about how easy it is to buy real estate with no down payment. I'm not saying it can't be done; however, I've been in this business for years and have yet to find a quality investment property that I could consider a good nothing-down deal. Most banks and savings and loans demand at least 20 percent down for investment property.

Foreclosures, government sales, and abandoned properties do exist; however, I'm not encouraged by any of these properties. I caution you to know exactly what you're doing and what you're getting into on the nothing-down real estate purchases.

Let me tell you of an experience I had with a nothing-down deal. This story happened a number of years ago, and I have to admit, I was rather naive at the time and didn't know too much about real estate. I had a couple of success stories under my belt and thought I was pretty smart and figured I could do no wrong. You know what I mean? Well let me tell you, I wasn't that smart and the investment deal did go wrong.

It turned out to be a lot of work and frustration. Here's what happened.

A local church group contacted me. One of their members had a Veteran's Administration (VA) mortgage home. He had lost his job and couldn't make the payments, but didn't want to have a foreclosure on his credit file. I was assured I could purchase the property, nothing down, and all I had to do was take over the payments.

Most VA loans are assumable, but VA will not borrow on investment property.

Sounds good? Nothing down, a simple and easy transaction, and I'm in business. On the surface it looked like a no-lose situation. Remember, I was pretty smart and could do no wrong.

I did go wrong. The deal was nowhere near as easy and simple as I had been led to believe. By the time the title was cleared, the abstract brought up to date, documents filed, and deed taxes and fees paid, I had to come up with about $1,000, and that's before even one payment was made.

That wasn't the end of it. The next thing I discovered was that the furnace went out and there was need of general repair work in the kitchen and bathroom. By the time this work was completed, I had spent another $5,000.

How'd I come out? Fortunately with time, that great ally of the real estate investor, I was able to come out ahead on the deal. I built up some equity from the rents and was able to realize some inflation. For the most part, I was able to recover my financial investment.

The point of this story is to let you know what I found out, and that is: *There's no such thing as something for nothing.* From this experience, I was able to learn that the nothing-down deals are more a myth than a reality. I also learned that I wasn't as smart as I thought. I didn't know it all and I had a lot to learn.

In conclusion, let me say this. Take your time, learn as much as possible about the real estate business, and be careful when you hear about a so-called nothing-down deal. Doesn't it make sense that money is going to change hands when property is purchased?

EQUITY SHARING IS AN
OPTION OF NOTHING-DOWN PURCHASES

One last word on nothing-down real estate. Equity sharing offers opportunities for buyers who have little or no cash. *Equity sharing* means buying property with a partner, someone who can and will finance the property. It's rather complicated and there's no reason to go into detail in this book. In fact, it's almost a book itself. If you're interested, I suggest you find out more information through another source.

When you bought this book, for all practical purposes, you started your career in real estate investing. The next step is up to you.

REAL ESTATE INVESTMENT MONEY IS AVAILABLE

By now you're probably saying, "How am I going to get money to finance investment property?" Well, take heart. There is money out there, and plenty of it. Let's take a look. Figure 6-1 shows a typical mortgage loan application.

Federal Housing Administration
Government-Guaranteed Loans

Let me start by telling you there isn't any such thing as a government loan, per se. The money comes from banks and savings and loans associations. The government guarantees the loan and if the borrower defaults on payments, the government pays off the mortgage holder. Applications for government-guaranteed loans are made through the banks and savings and loans, not through the government.

Getting a government-guaranteed loan involves a lot of red tape. If you've ever applied for a government loan, you know it's not all that easy. It can take some extra energy, a lot of time, and plenty of patience.

To qualify for a government-guaranteed loan, it's necessary to fill out many forms. Some information takes time to search out, so it's best to start early. Let's look at what's needed:

• Two years employment history is required, verified by your employer. The two years must be in related fields. One year as a banker and one year as an insurance salesman does not qualify.

• Two years income is required, verified by your employer, along with two years of W-2 forms. Self-employed applicants must provide two years of income tax returns.

• A complete financial statement, including all bills and obligations, loans, and credit card debts with current balances is required. The financial report must include all assets, liabilities, and obligations.

• A copy of your drivers license and social security card is required.

• A professional property appraisal is necessary.

• A credit bureau credit report must be provided.

Expect Snags and Save Yourself Headaches. About the time you think your application is going along fairly well, suddenly something

*Mortgage Loan
Application*

This application is designed to be completed by the Borrower(s) with the lender's assistance. The Co-Borrower Section and all other Co-Borrower questions must be completed and the appropriate box(es) checked if ☐ **another person will be jointly obligated with the Borrower on the loan, or** ☐ **the Borrower is relying on income from alimony, child support or separate maintenance or on the income or assets of another person as a basis for repayment of the loan,** or ☐ the Borrower is married and resides, or the property is located, in a community property state.

Borrower	**Co-Borrower**
B003 **Name** (last) _____	B006 **Name** (last) _____
B002 (first, middle initial) _____	3005 (first, middle initial) _____
	B470 B471		B478 B479
B101 Age ____ B102 Yrs. of school ____ ☐ M ☐ F	B116 Age ____ B117 Yrs. of school ____ ☐ M ☐ F
B105 **Current** address _____	B120 **Current** address _____
B106 City, state, zip _____	B121 City, state, zip _____
B103 B110	B124 B125
Dates from ____ to ____ No. Yrs. ____ ☐Rent ☐Own	Dates from ____ to ____ No. Yrs. ____ ☐ Rent ☐ Own
B107 **Previous** street address _____	B122 **Previous** street address _____
B108 City, state, zip _____	B123 City, state, zip _____
Dates from ____ to ____ No. Yrs. ____ ☐Rent ☐Own	Dates from ____ to ____ No. Yrs. ____ ☐ Rent ☐ Own
Previous street address _____	**Previous** street address _____
City, state, zip _____	City, state, zip _____
Dates from ____ to ____ No. Yrs. ____ ☐Rent ☐Own	Dates from ____ to ____ No. Yrs. ____ ☐ Rent ☐ Own
B111 ☐ Married B112 ☐ Unmarried B113 ☐ Separated	B111 ☐ Married B112 ☐ Unmarried B113 ☐ Separated
Former other name _____	Former other name _____
B114 Total # dependents ____ B115 Ages ____	B129 Total # dependents ____ B130 Ages ____
B131 **Employer** name _____	B142 **Employer** name _____
B132 Employer street address _____	B143 Employer street address _____
B133 City, state, zip _____	B144 City, state, zip _____
Person to contact _____	Person to contact _____
B135 B136	B135 B136
B134 Yrs. profession ____ Yrs. job ____ Self empl. ☐ Y ☐ N	B145 Yrs. profession ____ Yrs. job ____ Self empl. ☐ Y ☐ N
B137 Position title _____	B148 Position title _____
B138 Type business _____	B149 Type business _____
B139 Social Security no. ____ Date of birth ____	B150 Social Security no. ____ Date of birth ____
B140 Home phone ____ B141 Business phone ____	B151 Home phone ____ B152 Business phone ____

Gross Monthly Income

B153 Base income _____	B154 Base income _____
B155 Overtime _____	B156 Overtime _____
B157 Bonuses _____	B158 Bonuses _____
B159 Commissions _____	B160 Commissions _____
B161 Dividends, interest _____	B162 Dividends, interest _____

Describe Other Income — (do not include second job or rental income in this section)

Notice: Alimony, child support, or separate maintenance income need not be revealed if the Borrower or Co-Borrower does not choose to have in considered as a basis for repaying this loan.

B163	
B164 **Monthly** amount _____	B169 Other income belongs to: ☐ Borrower ☐ Co-borrower ☐ Both
B170 Description _____	
B165	
B166 **Monthly** amount _____	B172 Other income belongs to: ☐ Borrower ☐ Co-borrower ☐ Both
B173 Description _____	
B167	
B168 **Monthly** amount _____	B175 Other income belongs to: ☐ Borrower ☐ Co-borrower ☐ Both
B176 Description _____	

Fig. 6-1. A mortgage loan application is a standard form and is used for all bank, FHA, and VA loans.

Other/Previous Employment — *Complete only if employed at current position less than two years or if you have secondary employment.*

B179 **Employer** name _____	B195 **Employer** name _____
B178 ☐ Borrower ☐ Co-borrower B183 Dates empl. ____ to ____	B194 ☐ Borrower ☐ Co-borrower B199 Dates empl. ____ to ____
B710 Employer street addresss _____	B714 Employer street address _____
B180 City, state _____ B711 Zip _____	B196 City, state _____ B715 Zip _____
B181 Type of business _____	B197 Type of business _____
B182 Position title _____ B185 Monthly salary ____	B198 Position title _____ B201 Monthly salary ____
B187 **Employer** name _____	B203 **Employer** name _____
B186 ☐ Borrower ☐ Co-borrower B191 Dates empl. ____ to ____	B202 ☐ Borrower ☐ Co-borrower B207 Dates empl. ____ to ____
B712 Employer street addresss _____	B716 Employer street address _____
B188 City, state _____ B713 Zip _____	B204 City, state _____ B717 Zip _____
B189 Type of business _____	B205 Type of business _____
B190 Position title _____ B193 Monthly salary ____	B206 Position title _____ B209 Monthly salary ____

Current Monthly Housing Expense

B210 Rent _____ Mtg. payment _____ Taxes _____ Ins. _____ B211 Total _____

B212 HOA dues _____ B213 Utilities _____ Other _____

These questions apply to both borrower and co-borrower — If a "yes" answer is given to a question in this column, explain on an attached sheet.

	Borrower Yes or No	Co-borrower Yes or No
Have you any outstanding judgments? In the last 7 years, have you been declared bankrupt?	B214 _____	B215 _____
Have you had property foreclosed upon or given title or deed in lieu thereof?	B216 _____	B217 _____
Are you co-maker or endorser on a note?	B218 _____	B219 _____
Are you a party in a law suiit?	B220 _____	B221 _____
Are you obligated to pay alimony, child support, or separate maintenance?	B222 _____	B223 _____
Is any part of the down payment borrowed?	B224 _____	B225 _____

Assets

This Statement and any applicable supporting schedules may be completed jointly by both Borrower and Co-borrower if their assets and liabilities are sufficiently joined so that the Statement can be meaningfully and fairly presented on a combined basis; otherwise separate Statements and Schedules are required (FHLMC 65A/FNMA 1003A).

Earnest money/cash deposit B285 Amount $ _____	B003 **Completed jointly** ☐ Yes ☐ No
B284 **Held by** _____	L017 **Source of downpayment** _____
B226 **Bank** name _____	B245 **Bank** name _____
B227 Street _____	B246 Street _____
B228 City, state, zip _____	B247 City, state, zip _____

Account type	Owner	Account number	Balance	Account type	Owner	Account number	Balance
B229 _____	B C J	_____	B232 $ _____	B248 _____	B C J	_____	B251 $ _____
B233 _____	B C J	_____	B236 $ _____	B252 _____	B C J	_____	B255 $ _____
B237 _____	B C J	_____	B240 $ _____	B256 _____	B C J	_____	B259 $ _____
B241 _____	B C J	_____	B244 $ _____	B260 _____	B C J	_____	B263 $ _____

B264 **Bank** name _____	I067 **Bank** name _____
B265 Street _____	I068 Street _____
B266 City, state, zip _____	I069 City, state, zip _____

Account type	Owner	Account number	Balance	Account type	Owner	Account number	Balance
B267 _____	B C J	_____	B270 $ _____	I070 _____	B C J	_____	I073 $ _____
B271 _____	B C J	_____	B274 $ _____	I074 _____	B C J	_____	I077 $ _____
B275 _____	B C J	_____	B278 $ _____	I078 _____	B C J	_____	I081 $ _____
B279 _____	B C J	_____	B282 $ _____	I082 _____	B C J	_____	I085 $ _____

Current Assets: Stocks, Bonds, etc. | **Automobiles**

B286 Gift letter _____ B C J B287 $ _____   B298 Year/make _____ B C J B299 Value $ _____

B288 _____ B C J B289 $ _____   B300 Year/make _____ B C J B301 Value $ _____

B290 _____ B C J B291 $ _____   Furniture/**Personal** Property B 302 Value $ _____

B292 _____ B C J B293 $ _____   **Other Assets** (itemize)

Total $ _____   B303 _____ B304 $ _____

Life Insurance-B294 Face Value _____ B295 Cash Value $ _____   B305 _____ B306 $ _____

Retirement Fund-Vested interest _____ B297 $ _____   B307 _____ B308 $ _____

Business Owned-Net worth _____ B297 $ _____   B309 _____ B310 $ _____

Real Estate Owned — If more than three properties are owned attach separate schedule.

B420 Address _____   B423 Value _____ B424 Mortgage balance _____

City, state, zip _____   Lender name _____

B421 ☐ Sold ☐ Current residence ☐ Pending sale ☐ Rented Owner B C J   Lender address _____

B422 Property type: ☐ Residential ☐ Land ☐ Farm   B425 Gross rental income _____ B426 Mortgage payment _____

☐ Apartment ☐ Commercial ☐ Condo   B427 Taxes, insurance, misc. expense _____

B428 Address _____   B431 Value _____ B432 Mortgage balance _____

City, state, zip _____   Lender name _____

B429 ☐ Sold ☐ Current residence ☐ Pending sale ☐ Rented Owner B C J   Lender address _____

B430 Property type: ☐ Residential ☐ Land ☐ Farm   B433 Gross rental income _____ B434 Mortgage payment _____

☐ Apartment ☐ Commercial ☐ Condo   B434 Taxes, insurance, misc. expense _____

B436 Address _____   B439 Value _____ B440 Mortgage balance _____

City, state, zip _____   Lender name _____

B437 ☐ Sold ☐ Current residence ☐ Pending sale ☐ Rented Owner B C J   Lender address _____

B438 Property type: ☐ Residential ☐ Land ☐ Farm   B441 Gross rental income _____ B442 Mortgage payment _____

☐ Apartment ☐ Commercial ☐ Condo   B443 Taxes, insurance, misc. expense _____

Comments

_____

_____

_____

Liabilities — The Bank considers a liability to be any monthly obligation which the applicants are required to pay on a regular and timely basis. Obligations considered liabilities for this application are: Auto Loan — Credit Cards — Life Insurance — Time Notes — Credit Union — Other Debts — Alimony/Child Support.

Name on account B C J Type of loan ☐ Installment ☐ Revolving   Name on account B C J Type of loan ☐ Installment ☐ Revolving

☐ Mortgage ☐ Auto ☐ Other   ☐ Mortgage ☐ Auto ☐ Other

Creditor name _____   Creditor name _____

Creditor address _____   Creditor address _____

City, state, zip _____   City, state, zip _____

Account number _____ ☐ To be paid prior to closing   Account number _____ ☐ To be paid prior to closing

Payment amount _____ Balance _____   Payment amount _____ Balance _____

Name on account B C J Type of loan ☐ Installment ☐ Revolving   Name on account B C J Type of loan ☐ Installment ☐ Revolving

☐ Mortgage ☐ Auto ☐ Other   ☐ Mortgage ☐ Auto ☐ Other

Creditor name _____   Creditor name _____

Creditor address _____   Creditor address _____

City, state, zip _____   City, state, zip _____

Account number _____ ☐ To be paid prior to closing   Account number _____ ☐ To be paid prior to closing

Payment amount _____ Balance _____   Payment amount _____ Balance _____

| Name on account B C J | Type of loan | ☐ Installment | ☐ Revolving |
| | ☐ Mortgage | ☐ Auto | ☐ Other |

Creditor name _____

Creditor address _____

City, state, zip _____

Account number _____ ☐ To be paid prior to closing

Payment amount _____ Balance _____

| Name on account B C J | Type of loan | ☐ Installment | ☐ Revolving |
| | ☐ Mortgage | ☐ Auto | ☐ Other |

Creditor name _____

Creditor address _____

City, state, zip _____

Account number _____ ☐ To be paid prior to closing

Payment amount _____ Balance _____

| Name on account B C J | Type of loan | ☐ Installment | ☐ Revolving |
| | ☐ Mortgage | ☐ Auto | ☐ Other |

Creditor name _____

Creditor address _____

City, state, zip _____

Account number _____ ☐ To be paid prior to closing

Payment amount _____ Balance _____

| Name on account B C J | Type of loan | ☐ Installment | ☐ Revolving |
| | ☐ Mortgage | ☐ Auto | ☐ Other |

Creditor name _____

Creditor address _____

City, state, zip _____

Account number _____ ☐ To be paid prior to closing

Payment amount _____ Balance _____

| Name on account B C J | Type of loan | ☐ Installment | ☐ Revolving |
| | ☐ Mortgage | ☐ Auto | ☐ Other |

Creditor name _____

Creditor address _____

City, state, zip _____

Account number _____ ☐ To be paid prior to closing

Payment amount _____ Balance _____

| Name on account B C J | Type of loan | ☐ Installment | ☐ Revolving |
| | ☐ Mortgage | ☐ Auto | ☐ Other |

Creditor name _____

Creditor address _____

City, state, zip _____

Account number _____ ☐ To be paid prior to closing

Payment amount _____ Balance _____

List Previous Credit References

	B-Borrower	C-Co-borrower	Creditor's namd and address	Account number	Purpose	Highest balance	Date paid
B445							
B451							
B457							

List any additional names under which credit has previously been received

☐ I (we) were given a copy of the good faith estimate of closing costs and a copy of the RESPA pamphlet.

AGREEMENT: The undersigned applies for the loan indicated in this application to be secured by a first mortgage or deed of trust on the property described herein, and represents that the property will not be used for any illegal or restricted purpose, and that all statements made in this application are true and are made for the purpose of obtaining the loan. Verification may be obtained from any source named in this application. The original or a copy of this application will be retained by the lender, even if the loan is not granted. **The undersigned ☐ intend or ☐ do not intend to occupy the property as their primary residence.**

I/we fully understand that it is a federal crime punishable by fine or imprisonment, or both, to knowingly make any false statements concerning any of the above facts as applicable under the provisions of Title 18, United States Code, Section 1014.

Borrower's signature	Date	Co-borrower's signature	Date

Information for Government Monitoring Purposes

The following information is requested by the Federal Government if this loan is related to a dwelling, in order to monitor the lender's compliance with equal credit opportunity and fair housing laws. You are not required to furnish this information, but are encouraged to do so. The law provides that a lender may neither discriminate on the basis of this information, nor on whether you choose to furnish it. However, if you choose not to furnish it, under Federal regulations this lender is required to note race and sex on the basis of visual observation or surname. If you do not wish to furnish the above information, please initial below.

Borrower: I do not wish to furnish this information (initials) _____   **Co-Borrower:** I do not wish to furnish this information (initials) _____

Race/national origin   **Sex**

☐ Amer. Indian,   ☐ Hispanic   ☐ Asian, Pacific Islander   ☐ Female
Alaskan Native
☐ White   ☐ Black   ☐ Other _____   ☐ Male
                                    (specify)

Race/national origin   **Sex**

☐ Amer. Indian,   ☐ Hispanic   ☐ Asian, Pacific Islander   ☐ Female
Alaskan Native
☐ White   ☐ Black   ☐ Other _____   ☐ Male
                                    (specify)

EQUAL HOUSING
LENDER

Remainder of Questionnaire for Interviewer Use Only

L055 **Appl. date** _____   *C010* **Estimated closing date** _____   *C007* **Sales price or est. value** _____

                                                    U322 **VA Funding fee**   *U323* **Loan amt. + MIP or**
C002 **Requested loan amount** _____   **or Financed MIP** _____   **Loan amt. + VA fee** _____   *C003* **Interest rate** _____

Loan type: ☐ *Assumption*   ☐ *GPM*   Plan _____   *C005* Amortized term _____
  ☐ *FHA*   ☐ *Conv. Ins.*   ☐ *ARM*   ☐ *Balloon*   *C006* Actual term _____
  ☐ *VA*   ☐ *Conv. Unins.* ☐ *EOM*   ☐ *Buydown*   ☐ *Permanent*   *B462* ☐ *Owner occupied*
                                 Other _____ ☐ *Temporary*   *B463* ☐ *Other* _____

Investor: ☐ *Investor*   ☐ *Purchase*   **Prepayment Penalty**
  ☐ *State Housing Program*   ☐ *Refinance*   *Z933* ☐ *Yes*   *Z004* ☐ *None*
  ☐ *Portfolio*   ☐ *Const/Perm*   **Estate:** ☐ *Leasehold* *Expires* _____
  ☐ *Other* _____   ☐ *Other* _____   ☐ *Fee Simple* ☐ *Other* _____

PMI company _____   ☐ *Level/renewal*   **Lien:** ☐ *1st mtg.* ☐ *Other (specify)* _____
Coverage _____ % 1st year premium _____ ☐ *Amortizing renewal*   **Title:** ☐ *Joint tenancy*   ☐ *Tenants-in-common*   ☐ *Individual*
☐ *Primary residence* ☐ *Second/vacation*   ☐ *Rural*   ☐ *Urban*
☐ _____   ☐ _____   **Loan to value** _____ % Is loan assumable? _____

Loan discount - Total _____ %   Investor _____   Purchase price .... $ _____
F104 **Buyer** _____ % or $ _____   Total closing costs (est.) .... + $ _____
F104 **Seller** _____ % or $ _____   Prepaid escrows (refinance) .... + $ _____
Discount reserved ____/____/ **Discount expires** ____/____/   Total .... = $ _____
Origination fee _____ %   Discount to Investor _____ %   Amount this mortgage .... − $ _____
VA funding fee _____ %   **ARM**   Other financing .... − $ _____
  Paid by ☐ *Vet* ☐ *Seller*   Index _____   Other equity .... − $ _____
  ☐ *No fee* ☐ *Disabled vet*   Margin _____   Amount of cash deposit .... − $ _____
Commitment fee _____ %   Closing costs paid by seller .... − $ _____
                                                                    Cash required for closing (est.) .... − $ _____

Gross income (monthly)

Borrower 1 $ _____   **Property address** _____
Borrower 2 $ _____   City, state, zip _____
Other income $ _____   County _____
Total $ _____   Number of units _____ Date built _____
P & I $ _____ _____ % Legal description: _____
Hazard insurance $ _____   _____
RE taxes $ _____   _____
Mortgage insurance $ _____   Census tract _____
Mortgage payment $ _____ _____ % **Seller's name** _____
Other $ _____   Address _____
Subtotal $ _____   City, state, zip _____ Phone _____
Other monthly debt $ _____ _____ % ☐ *Individual*   ☐ *Husband & wife*   ☐ *Other*
Mtg. pmt. & other debt $ _____ _____ %

L059 **Listing realtor**   *L060* **Selling realtor**
Salesperson _____   Salesperson _____
Firm _____   Firm _____
Phone _____   Phone _____

Appraisal data: Occupant — ☐ *Owner* ☐ *Tenant* ☐ *Vacant*   Case number _____
Contact for inspection: _____   Phone number _____
Available for inspection: _____ a.m. _____ p.m. Keys at _____
Appraiser requested _____   Instructions to appraiser _____

Comments _____

_____

_____

_____

_____

_____

_____

For Lender's Use Only _____

(FNMA REQUIREMENT ONLY) This application was taken by ☐ *face to face interview*   ☐ *by mail*   ☐ *by telephone*   *Date* _____

_____   _____

Members FDIC (interviewer)   *Name of employer or interviewer*

_____   _____

Bank representative   *Bank name location*

turns up and takes more time and work. Here's an example of what I mean.

A friend of mine applied for a government-guaranteed loan. Included in the application was the fact that he owned some limited-partnership oil stock. Before the loan could be processed, he had to acquire a financial statement from the oil company, despite the fact that he had no financial or legal liability.

Things like that take time and sometimes can be irritating. Expect this red tape to happen and save that irritation.

One learns the value of time, good or bad, in the real estate business.

Most Federal Housing Administration (FHA) applications will take from 90 to 120 days to complete—sometimes longer. Be prepared.

Now that you know time is involved and most loan applications involve time, here's some advice. Stipulate in the purchase agreement, that if there are unsolvable difficulties and circumstances, you can get out of the agreement without it costing you anything.

Be Aware of Unforeseen Costs. For you to qualify for a government-guaranteed loan, the property must be appraised. The cost of this appraisal is about $100, but in some cases it can be more.

What's important to know is that if the appraiser indicates repairs need to be made on the property before the loan will be approved, the question is, who pays? In all probability, the loan will not include the costs of these repairs. Therefore, it's necessary to have a stipulation in writing and in the purchase agreement of who pays any additional costs.

Another restriction is that if you own five or more properties in one community, including a personal home, the government will not approve a guaranteed loan. Don't ask me why.

Some restrictions can depend on your financial status, others on the property itself. Be aware of the various inconveniences and problems you might encounter. It's a lot easier to tolerate the government red tape if you know it's there ahead of time.

I think it's safe to say you'll receive competent help from your banker in getting the application for a government loan. Bankers know the procedure.

Now it's time to get back to the actual source of the money: bankers, savings and loans, and sellers. From now on, I'll refer to all loaning institutions as *bankers*.

Confronting the Banker for Money

Over the years I've had a pretty good relationship with bankers, and you should feel good about the relationship you have with your banker when you go for a loan. It's a matter of understanding and knowing what the bank is there for; to make loans for profit.

Most bankers aren't any different than you and me. They aren't that difficult to get along with. Bankers are pretty much down-to-earth people, just like you and me, and some are even our neighbors.

However, the fact is that the banker has one job and that is to make a good loan, be sure he gets payments, and makes a profit for the bank. To make this money he's going to ask for as much security as he can. Our first step then will be to establish bank security, or *borrowing power*.

Check Your Inventory of Borrowing Power

If you're reading this book you probably have more security and borrowing power than you realize. Following is a list of what we might call *money power* because that's what security is:

- A good credit rating
- Equity in real estate
- Stocks, savings, bonds
- Life insurance equity or cash value
- Pension funds
- Personal property
- Job longevity
- Earning power

All of these items represent security. There's one ironic thing about security and that is the old saying, "If you've got money, you can make money." The problem with most of us is which comes first, the chicken or the egg. How do we get that money in the first place? This question is important especially for the young, beginning investor.

A good credit record is very important, and must be one of the first steps the beginning investor takes. I think it's safe to say that if you're overloaded with debt, you don't have sufficient income to make payments, and if you have a bad credit rating, you're not going to get the banker's attention.

If we go on the assumption that you have some stability, some security, and a good credit rating, we can start with the banker. Any one of the previously mentioned assets should be enough to get you started with most bankers. This list pretty much represents the security they need, and let me tell you, security impresses bankers.

You can enhance that impression by preparing yourself well before making your initial interview. Here's how. The banker likes to deal with people who are well organized.

Prepare your financial statement with vigor. (Fig. 6-2 and Fig. 6-3 are examples of typical personal financial statements.) Show all your assets as follows—in written form:

- Home
- Investment real estate
- Cabin
- Savings
- Stocks
- Bonds
- Insurance cash value
- Household goods
- Cars
- Personal property

Also, have a list of liabilities and payments:

- Home mortgage
- Car mortgage
- Credit card balances
- Personal loan balances
- Insurance loan balances
- All outstanding debts and obligations

Personal
Financial Statement

To: _____

*If I have any questions regarding the completion of this
form, I should contact my representative at the bank.*

*I may apply for a credit extension, loan or other financial accommodation alone or together with someone else,
("co-applicant"). If I apply with a co-applicant and our combined assets and debts can meaningfully and fairly be
presented together, the co-applicant and I may complete this required statement and any supporting schedules
jointly. Otherwise, separate forms and schedules are required.*

APPLICANT

Name _____   Social Security number _____

Address _____

Telephone number _____   Date of birth _____

Present employer _____   Position _____

Address _____

Business phone _____   Loan purpose _____

CO-APPLICANT

Name _____   Social Security number _____

Address _____

Telephone number _____   Date of birth _____

Present employer _____   Position _____

Address _____

Business phone _____   Loan purpose _____

Fig. 6-2. A personal financial statement.

Date of valuation

● Round all amounts to the nearest $100
● Attach separate sheet if you need more space to complete detail schedule

Assets (assets you own)	Amount	Liabilities (debts you owe)	Amount
Cash in this bank: Checking		Loans payable to banks (schedule 7)	
Savings		Loans payable to others (schedule 7)	
C.D.s		Installment contracts payable (schedule 7)	
IRA		Amounts due to dept. stores and others	
Cash in other banks		Credit cards (MasterCard, Visa & others)	
Due from friends, relatives and others (schedule 1)		Income taxes payable	
Mortgage and contracts for deed owned (schedule 2)		Other taxes payable	
Securities owned (schedule 3)			
Cash surrender value of life insurance (schedule 4)		Loans on life insurance (schedule 4)	
Homestead (schedule 5)			
Other real estate owned (schedule 5)		Mortgage on homestead (schedule 6)	
Automobiles (year, make, model)		Mortgage or liens on other real estate owned (schedule 6)	
		Contracts for deed (schedule 6)	
Personal property			
		Other liabilities (detail)	
Other assets (detail)			
		TOTAL LIABILITIES	
		Net worth (total assets less total liabilities)	
TOTAL		TOTAL	

Annual income	Applicant	Co-applicant	Contingent liabilities	Amount
Salary			As endorser	
Commissions			As guarantor	
Dividends			Lawsuits	
Interest			For taxes	
Rentals			Other (detail)	
Alimony, child support or maintenance (you need not show this unless you wish us to consider it).				
Other				
			☐ Check here if "none"	
TOTAL INCOME			TOTAL CONTINGENT LIABILITIES	

SCHEDULE 1 DUE FROM FRIENDS, RELATIVES AND OTHERS

Name of debtor	Owed to	Collateral	How payable	Maturity date	Unpaid balance
			$ per		
			$ per		
			$ per		
				TOTAL	

SCHEDULE 2 MORTGAGE AND CONTRACTS FOR DEED OWNED

Name of debtor	Type of property	1st or 2nd lien	Owed to	How payable	Unpaid balance
				$ per	
				$ per	
				$ per	
				$ per	
				TOTAL	

SCHEDULE 3 SECURITIES OWNED

No. shares or Bond amount	Description	In whose name(s) registered	Cost	Present Market value	L-listed U-unlisted
		TOTAL			

SCHEDULE 4 LIFE INSURANCE

Insured	Insurance company	Beneficiary	Face value of policy	Cash value	Loans
		TOTAL			

SCHEDULE 5 REAL ESTATE

Address and type of property	Title in name(s) of	Monthly Income	Cost Year acquired	Present Market value	Amount of Insurance
Homestead			$ _____ Year		
			$ _____ Year		
			$ _____ Year		
			$ _____ Year		
			$ _____ Year		

SCHEDULE 6 MORTGAGES OR LIENS ON REAL ESTATE

To whom payable	How payable	Interest Rate	Maturity Date	Unpaid Balance
Homestead	$ _____ per			
	$ _____ per			
	$ _____ per			
	$ _____ per			
	$ _____ per			

SCHEDULE 7 LOANS PAYABLE TO BANKS & OTHERS AND INSTALLMENT CONTRACTS PAYABLE

To whom payable	Address	Collateral or Unsecured	How payable	Maturity Date	Unpaid Balance
			$ _____ per		
			$ _____ per		
			$ _____ per		
			$ _____ per		
			$ _____ per		
			$ _____ per		
			$ _____ per		
			$ _____ per		

	APPLICANT	CO-APPLICANT
Have I ever gone through bankruptcy or had a judgment against me?	☐ Yes ☐ No	☐ Yes ☐ No
Are any assets pledged or debts secured except as shown?	☐ Yes ☐ No	☐ Yes ☐ No
Have I made a will?	☐ Yes ☐ No	☐ Yes ☐ No
Number of dependents (if none, check ''None'')	_____ ☐ None	_____ ☐ None
Marital status (answer only if this financial statement is provided in connection with a request for secured credit or applicant is seeking a joint account with spouse.)	☐ Married ☐ Separated ☐ Unmarried	☐ Married ☐ Separated ☐ Unmarried

(Unmarried includes single, divorced, widowed)

The foregoing statement, submitted for the purpose of obtaining credit, is true and correct in every detail and fairly shows my/our financial condition at the time indicated. I/we will give you prompt written notice of any subsequent substantial change in such financial condition occurring before discharge of my/our obligations to you. I/we understand that you will retain this personal financial statement whether or not you approve the credit in connection with which it is submitted. You are authorized to check my/our credit and employment history or any other information contained herein.

THE UNDERSIGNED CERTIFY THAT THE INFORMATION CONTAINED ON THIS
FORM HAS BEEN CAREFULLY REVIEWED AND THAT IT IS TRUE AND CORRECT IN ALL RESPECTS.

_____   _____
Date   My signature

_____   _____
Date   Co-applicant signature (if you are requesting the financial accommodation jointly)

TO _____

TYPE OF CREDIT — CHECK THE APPROPRIATE BOX   (Name of Lender)

☐ Individual — If you check this box, provide Financial Information only about yourself.

☐ Joint, with _____ Relationship _____ If you check this box, provide Financial Information about
     yourself and the other person.

PERSONAL FINANCIAL STATEMENT OF

NOTE: Any willful misrepresentation could result in a violation of Federal Law (Sec. 18 U.S.C. 1014)

Name _____ Birth Date _____ , 19___ Statement Date _____ , 19___

Address _____ City _____ State/Zip _____ Social Sec. No. _____

Home Phone _____ No. of Dependents _____ Bus. or Occupation _____ Bus. Phone _____

NOTE: Complete all of Section II BEFORE Section I

SECTION I

ASSETS		THOU-SANDS	HUN-DREDS	CENTS	LIABILITIES		THOU-SANDS	HUN-DREDS	CENTS
1 Cash On Hand & in Banks	Sec. II-A				21 Notes Due to Banks	Sec. II-A			
2 Cash Value of Life Insurance	Sec. II-B				22 Notes Due to Relatives & Friends	Sec. II-H			
3 U.S. Gov. Securities	Sec. II-C				23 Notes Due to Others	Sec. II-H			
4 Other Marketable Securities	Sec. II-C				24 Accounts & Bills Payable	Sec. II-H			
5 Notes & Accounts Receivable - Good	Sec. II-D				25 Unpaid Income Taxes Due - ☐ Federal ☐ State				
6 Other Assets Readily Convertible to Cash - Itemize					26 Other Unpaid Taxes & Interest				
7					27 Loans on Life Insurance Policies	Sec. II-B			
8					28 Contract Accounts Payable	Sec. II-H			
9					29 Cash Rent Owed				
10 TOTAL CURRENT ASSETS					30 Other Liabilities Due within 1 Year - Itemize				
11 Real Estate Owned	Sec. II-E				31				
12 Mortgages & Contracts Owned	Sec. II-F				32				
13 Notes & Accounts Receivable - Doubtful	Sec. II-D				33 TOTAL CURRENT LIABILITIES				
14 Notes Due From Relatives & Friends	Sec. II-D				34 Real Estate Mortgages Payable	Sec. II-E			
15 Other Securities - Not Readily Marketable	Sec. II-C				35 Liens & Assessments Payable				
16 Personal Property	Sec. II-G				36 Other Debts - Itemize				
17 Other Assets - Itemize					37				
18					38 Total Liabilities				
19					39 Net Worth (Total Assets minus Total Liabilities)				
20 TOTAL ASSETS					40 TOTAL LIABILITIES & NET WORTH				

ANNUAL INCOME		ESTIMATE OF ANNUAL EXPENSES	
Salary, Bonuses & Commissions	$	Income Taxes	$
Dividends & Interest	$	Other Taxes	$
Rental & Lease Income (Net)	$	Insurance Premiums	$
Alimony, child support, or separate maintenance income need not be revealed if you do not wish to have it considered as a basis for repaying this obligation. Other Income—Itemize	$	Mortgage Payments	$
		Rent Payable	$
Provide the following information only if Joint Credit is checked above.		Other Expenses	$
Other Persons Salary, Bonuses & Commissions	$		$
Alimony, child support, or separate maintenance income need not be revealed if you do not wish to have it considered as a basis for repaying this obligation. Other Income of Other Person—Itemize	$		$
			$
TOTAL	$	TOTAL	$

GENERAL INFORMATION	CONTINGENT LIABILITIES	
Are any Assets Pledged? ☐ No ☐ Yes (See Section II)	As Endorser, Co-maker or Guarantor	$
Are you a Defendant in any Suits or Legal Actions? ☐ No ☐ Yes	On Leases or Contracts	$
(Explain):	Legal Claims	$
Have you ever been declared Bankrupt in the last 10 years? ☐ No ☐ Yes	Federal - State Income Taxes	$
(Explain):	Other -	$

SECTION II

A   CASH IN BANKS AND NOTES DUE TO BANKS   (List all Real Estate Loans in Section II-E)

NAME OF BANK	Type of Account	Type of Ownership	On Deposit	Notes Due Banks	COLLATERAL (If Any) & Type of Ownership
			$	$	
		Cash on Hand	$		
(Complete Rest of Section II on Reverse Side)		TOTALS	$	$	
			(Enter Sec. I Line 1)	(Enter Sec. I Line 21)	

BANKERS SYSTEMS. INC. ST. CLOUD. MINNESOTA
FORM PS-15   7-25-84

Fig. 6-3. Personal financial statements give you some idea of what type information is needed so the bank will process a real estate loan. Look them over. Go to your banker and ask for their application.

SECTION II Continued

B   LIFE INSURANCE   (List only those Policies that you own)

COMPANY	Face of Policy	Cash Surrender Value	Policy Loan from Insurance Co	Other Loans Policy as Collateral	BENEFICIARY
	$	$	$	$	
TOTALS	$		$		
	(Enter Sec. 1 Line 2)		(Enter Sec. 1 Line 27)		

C   SECURITIES OWNED   (Including U.S. Gov't Bonds and all other Stocks and Bonds)

Face Value Bonds No. of Shares Stock	DESCRIPTION Indicate those Not Registered in Your Name	Type of Ownership	COST	Market Value U S Gov Sec	Market Value Marketable Sec	MARKET VALUE Not Readily Marketable SECURITIES	Amount Pledged to Secured Loans
							$
		TOTALS	$		$	$	
			(Enter Sec. 1 Line 3)		(Enter Sec. 1 Line 4)	(Enter Sec. 1 Line 15)	

D   NOTES AND ACCOUNTS RECEIVABLE   (Money Payable or Owed to You Individually-Indicate by a ✔ if Others have an Ownership Interest)

MAKER DEBTOR	✔	When Due	Original Amount	Balance Due Good Accounts	Balance Due Doubtful Accounts	Bal Due Notes Rel & Friends	SECURITY (If Any)
			$	$	$	$	
		TOTALS	$	$	$		
			(Enter Sec. 1 Line 5)	(Enter Sec. 1 Line 13)	(Enter Sec. 1 Line 14)		

E   REAL ESTATE OWNED   (Indicate by a ✔ if Others have an Ownership Interest)

TITLE IN NAME OF	✔	Description & Location	Date Acquired	Original Cost	Present Value of Real Estate	Amount of Ins Carried	MORTGAGE OR CONTRACT PAYABLE			
							Bal Due	Payment	Maturity	To Whom Payable
Homestead				$	$	$				
			TOTAL	$		TOTAL	$			
				(Enter Sec. 1 Line 11)			(Enter Sec. 1 Line 34)			

F   MORTGAGES AND CONTRACTS OWNED   (Indicate by a ✔ if Others have an Ownership Interest)

Cont	Mtge	✔	MAKER Name	Address	PROPERTY COVERED	Starting Date	Payment	Maturity	Balance Due
							$		$
							TOTALS	$	
								(Enter Sec. 1 Line 12)	

G   PERSONAL PROPERTY   (Indicate by a ✔ if Others have an Ownership Interest)

DESCRIPTION	✔	Date When New	Cost When New	Value Today	LOANS ON PROPERTY	
					Balance Due	To Whom Payable
Automobiles			$	$	$	
		TOTAL	$			
			(Enter Sec. 1 Line 16)			

H   NOTES   (Other than Bank, Mortgage and Insurance Company Loans).   ACCOUNTS AND BILLS AND CONTRACTS PAYABLE

PAYABLE TO	Other Obligors (If Any)	When Due	Notes Due To Rel & Friends	Notes Due 'Others' (Not Banks)	Accounts & Bills Payable	Contracts Payable	COLLATERAL (If Any)
			$				
		TOTALS	$				
			(Enter Sec. 1 Line 22)	(Enter Sec. 1 Line 23)	(Enter Sec. 1 Line 24)	(Enter Sec. 1 Line 28)	

For the purpose of procuring credit from time to time I We furnish the foregoing as a true and accurate statement of my our financial condition Authorization is hereby given to the Lender to verify in any manner it deems appropriate any and all items indicated on this statement The undersigned also agrees to notify the Lender immediately in writing of any significant adverse change in such financial condition

Date Signed_____, 19____ Signature _____   Signature _____

(Other Person if Applicable)

Prepare a complete report of your earning power:

- Salary and commissions
- Additional family income
- Investment income
- Financial gifts
- Future inheritances

Then prepare a complete report of the property with the following information included:

- Location and description
- Type of property (duplex four-plex, etc.)
- Price
- Rental income
- Taxes, insurance, upkeep

If the property has sufficient income to cash flow, be sure to call this fact to the attention of the banker.

Then let the banker know what you want:

- Amount of loan
- Length and terms of loan
- Payment schedule
- Estimated interest

Although the banker will most likely order his own credit report, have one of your own ready for him. Go to the credit bureau and buy your own report. In this way, the banker will know you mean business and know what you're doing.

Then present yourself, with all your information, in a very businesslike manner. The day you make your presentation, dress up. Look sharp, act sharp, and be sharp. This presentation is almost like a job interview in that you're about to go into one of the most dynamic businesses there is: real estate. Real estate investing could be your job for the rest of your life.

One last word: be positive and assertive. Don't be wishy-washy.

How to Avoid Paying Points and Higher Interest

Remember, I said that being assertive in the real estate business is important. You can use that assertiveness in dealing with the banker on points and interest.

All banks don't charge points and all customers don't pay points. Does this surprise you? It shouldn't, because it's a fact. Wealthy people don't pay points, people with borrowing power don't pay points, and I don't pay points. Small-town banks sometimes don't charge points.

There's one other way of not paying points, and that is by being willing to pay a higher rate of interest on the loan. Sometimes this can be the best way, especially when you are dealing with investment property. I say this because usually if you're buying property all the time you're refinancing all the time. Here's an example of what I mean.

A friend of mine bought a property and financed it with a long-term mortgage. He made the payments for about five years and then decided to buy more property. He had some equity in this first property so the old mortgage was scrapped.

As you get into the business, you'll find you're constantly refinancing, making out new loans, and paying off old ones. As you analyze your loans and want to avoid those points, pay a higher rate of interest right from the start.

Incidentally, interest rates, like points, vary from bank to bank. As you shop for financing, check with all the various loaning institutions before making a final decision.

Tell your banker you're not interested in paying points. Here's another situation where being assertive pays off. Come right out with it and tell the banker you want a loan and you're not excited about paying him points. Tell this to each and every contact you make. Some will laugh at you, some will take you seriously, and some will give you a loan without points.

Chisel; work one bank against the other. Tell them you've got a better deal down the street or out of town. Use whatever money power you have to negotiate your loan. And whatever, don't beg or grovel.

The Contract-for-Deed Financing

The next source of financing is the seller, better known as the *contract for deed*. I personally find this source one of the best for investment property. In fact, because of its importance, the next chapter covers the contract for deed in detail.

7

The
Contract for Deed
and Other Contracts

FOR THE SMALL BEGINNING INVESTOR, THIS CHAPTER IS PROBABLY THE most important chapter of the entire book. Here's why.

I believe the contract for deed is the easiest, least expensive, and most reliable method for the average person to buy investment real estate. It is, in my mind, the key to starting most small investors in the real estate business, especially those who don't have the borrowing power or the money to qualify for conventional bank financing.

The contract for deed is a simple, legal document, sometimes called an *installment contract*. What it amounts to is this. The buyer agrees to pay a certain amount for the property. Let's say, using a hypothetical case, the property sells for $100,000. If the contract is written for 25 years, no down payment, and a 9 percent interest rate, the buyer will pay $827.98 per month for 25 years. When the contract is paid in full, the title of the property is then transferred to the buyer.

Always have an attorney represent you when you are transacting a contract-for-deed purchase, or any other real estate deed for that matter.

With a traditional mortgage, the title of the property is transferred at the time of purchase, rather than at the end of the payment period as with the terms of a contract for deed. Contract-for-deed conditions differ from other financed purchases; however, this is the basic difference. Figure 7-1 illustrates a typical contract for deed.

The contract-for-deed purchase is comparatively easy; it's quick and inexpensive. The down payment is totally negotiable between the buyer and seller and can be any amount upon which they agree.

Points are not paid on a contract for deed. The interest, like the down payment, is totally negotiable. No waiting occurs in a contract for deed. No forms need to be filled out and the entire transaction and contract can be completed within a matter of hours.

NEGOTIATING A CONTRACT-FOR-DEED PURCHASE

Obviously the first thing in negotiating a contract for deed is to find a seller who is willing to negotiate the contract. This search can be done through real estate agents, as well as through direct contact with sellers.

The first thing to do is let your real estate agents know you're interested in buying on a contract for deed so they can start looking for properties. You might want to consider going to several agencies. Call the agents periodically because sometimes they can overlook you and forget your interests. In fact, I've made it a point to become casual friends with several agents, have coffee with them periodically. In this way, they look after my interests.

In addition to real estate agents, of course there's the individual seller. Watch the newspaper advertisements, as well as yards signs for these sellers.

Also, contact other investors. If there's an apartment owners association in your community, you might join and meet other investors. I've bought over 80 percent of my holdings from other investors, and most of this property was never listed with a real estate agency.

The next step, of course, is ask the seller if he'll take a contract for deed. I'm convinced a lot of sellers are interested in a contract for deed, if they find the right person with the right credentials and are asked. At first you'll probably hear, "No, I want a cash sale." But I have a feeling once a communication is set up and the seller finds you dependable, he'll change his mind.

Usually the contract-for-deed sellers are just plain, ordinary people who've probably been in the real estate business for a number of years and now want out. They want to sell to an investor who is going to take care of the property and make the monthly payment.

I've found that most sellers have their property paid off. Therefore, if they sell on a contract for deed, they eliminate the management problems of the property, they can earn interest on their investment with the monthly payment, and they sit back and watch their money grow—

CONTRACT FOR DEED

Individual Seller

No delinquent taxes and transfer entered;
Certificate of Real Estate Value
( )filed ( )not required
_____ , 19___ .

_____
County Auditor

By _____
Deputy

(reserved for mortgage registry tax payment data)

(reserved for recording data)

MORTGAGE REGISTRY TAX DUE HEREON:

$_____

Date: _____ , 19___

THIS CONTRACT FOR DEED is made on the above date by _____

_____ , _____ ,
(marital status)

Seller (whether one or more), and _____

_____ , Purchaser (whether one or more).

Seller and Purchaser agree to the following terms:

1. PROPERTY DESCRIPTION. Seller hereby sells, and Purchaser hereby buys, real property in
_____ County, _____ , described as follows:

together with all hereditaments and appurtenances belonging thereto (the Property).

Fig. 7-1. A routine contract for deed.

2. TITLE. Seller warrants that title to the Property is, on the date of this contract, subject only to the following exceptions:
   (a) Covenants, conditions, restrictions, declarations and easements of record, if any;
   (b) Reservations of minerals or mineral rights by the State of Minnesota, if any;
   (c) Building, zoning and subdivision laws and regulations;
   (d) The lien of real estate taxes and installments of special assessments which are payable by Purchaser pursuant to paragraph 6 of this contract; and
   (e) The following liens or encumbrances:

3. DELIVERY OF DEED AND EVIDENCE OF TITLE. Upon Purchaser's prompt and full performance of this contract, Seller shall:
   (a) Execute, acknowledge and deliver to Purchaser a _____ Deed, in recordable form, conveying marketable title to the Property to Purchaser, subject only to the following exceptions:
       (i) Those exceptions referred to in paragraph 2(a), (b), (c) and (d) of this contract;
       (ii) Liens, encumbrances, adverse claims or other matters which Purchaser has created, suffered or permitted to accrue after the date of this contract; and
       (iii) The following liens or encumbrances:

                                                                                          ; and

   (b) Deliver to Purchaser the abstract of title to the Property or, if the title is registered, the owner's duplicate certificate of title.

4. PURCHASE PRICE. Purchaser shall pay to Seller, at _____ _____ , the sum of _____ ($_____) , as and for the purchase price for the Property, payable as follows:

5. PREPAYMENT. Unless otherwise provided in this contract, Purchaser shall have the right to fully or partially prepay this contract at any time without penalty. Any partial prepayment shall be applied first to payment of amounts then due under this contract, including unpaid accrued interest, and the balance shall be applied to the principal installments to be paid in the inverse order of their maturity. Partial prepayment shall not postpone the due date of the installments to be paid pursuant to this contract or change the amount of such installments.

6. REAL ESTATE TAXES AND ASSESSMENTS. Purchaser shall pay, before penalty accrues, all real estate taxes and installments of special assessments assessed against the Property which are due and payable in the year 19___ and in all subsequent years. Real estate taxes and installments of special assessments which are due and payable in the year in which this contract is dated shall be paid as follows:

Seller warrants that the real estate taxes and installments of special assessments which were due and payable in the years preceding the year in which this contract is dated are paid in full.

7. PROPERTY INSURANCE.
    (a) INSURED RISKS AND AMOUNT. Purchaser shall keep all buildings, improvements and fixtures now or later located on or a part of the Property insured against loss by fire, extended coverage perils, vandalism, malicious mischief and, if applicable, steam boiler explosion for at least the amount of _____ .
    If any of the buildings, improvements or fixtures are located in a federally designated flood prone area, and if flood insurance is available for that area, Purchaser shall procure and maintain flood insurance in amounts reasonably satisfactory to Seller.
    (b) OTHER TERMS. The insurance policy shall contain a loss payable clause in favor of Seller which provides that Seller's right to recover under the insurance shall not be impaired by any acts or omissions of Purchaser or Seller, and that Seller shall otherwise be afforded all rights and privileges customarily provided a mortgagee under the so-called standard mortgage clause.
    (c) NOTICE OF DAMAGE. In the event of damage to the Property by fire or other casualty, Purchaser shall promptly give notice of such damage to Seller and the insurance company.

8. DAMAGE TO THE PROPERTY.
    (a) APPLICATION OF INSURANCE PROCEEDS. If the Property is damaged by fire or other casualty, the insurance proceeds paid on account of such damage shall be applied to payment of the amounts payable by Purchaser under this contract, even if such amounts are not then due to be paid, unless Purchaser makes a permitted election described in the next paragraph. Such amounts shall be first applied to unpaid accrued interest and next to the installments to be paid as provided in this contract in the inverse order of their maturity. Such payment shall not postpone the due date of the installments to be paid pursuant to this contract or change the amount of such installments. The balance of insurance proceeds, if any, shall be the property of Purchaser.
    (b) PURCHASER'S ELECTION TO REBUILD. If Purchaser is not in default under this contract, or after curing any such default, and if the mortgagees in any prior mortgages and sellers in any prior contracts for deed do not require otherwise, Purchaser may elect to have that portion of such insurance proceeds necessary to repair, replace or restore the damaged Property (the repair work) deposited in escrow with a bank or title insurance company qualified to do business in the State of Minnesota, or such other party as may be mutually agreeable to Seller and Purchaser. The election may only be made by written notice to Seller within sixty days after the damage occurs. Also, the election will only be permitted if the plans and specifications and contracts for the repair work are approved by Seller, which approval Seller shall not unreasonably withhold or delay. If such a permitted election is made by Purchaser, Seller and Purchaser shall jointly deposit, when paid, such insurance proceeds into such escrow. If such insurance proceeds are insufficient for the repair work, Purchaser shall, before the commencement of the repair work, deposit into such escrow sufficient additional money to insure the full payment for the repair work. Even if the insurance proceeds are unavailable or are insufficient to pay the cost of the repair work, Purchaser shall at all times be responsible to pay the full cost of the repair work. All escrowed funds shall be disbursed by the escrowee in accordance with generally accepted sound construction disbursement procedures. The costs incurred or to be incurred on account of such escrow shall be deposited by Purchaser into such escrow before the commencement of the repair work. Purchaser shall complete the repair work as soon as reasonably possible and in a good and workmanlike manner, and in any event the repair work shall be completed by Purchaser within one year after the damage occurs. If, following the completion of and payment for the repair work, there remain any undisbursed escrow funds, such funds shall be applied to payment of the amounts payable by Purchaser under this contract in accordance with paragraph 8 (a) above.

9. INJURY OR DAMAGE OCCURRING ON THE PROPERTY.
    (a) LIABILITY. Seller shall be free from liability and claims for damages by reason of injuries occurring on or after the date of this contract to any person or persons or property while on or about the Property. Purchaser shall defend and indemnify Seller from all liability, loss, costs and obligations, including reasonable attorneys' fees, on account of or arising out of any such injuries. However, Purchaser shall have no liability or obligation to Seller for such injuries which are caused by the negligence or intentional wrongful acts or omissions of Seller.
    (b) LIABILITY INSURANCE. Purchaser shall, at Purchaser's own expense, procure and maintain liability insurance against claims for bodily injury, death and property damage occuring on or about the Property in amounts reasonably satisfactory to Seller and naming Seller as an additional insured.

10. INSURANCE, GENERALLY. The insurance which Purchaser is required to procure and maintain pursuant to paragraphs 7 and 9 of this contract shall be issued by an insurance company or companies licensed to do business in the State of Minnesota and acceptable to Seller. The insurance shall be maintained by Purchaser at all times while any amount remains unpaid under this contract. The insurance policies shall provide for not less than ten days written notice to Seller before cancellation, non-renewal, termination or change in coverage, and Purchaser shall deliver to Seller a duplicate original or certificate of such insurance policy or policies.

11. CONDEMNATION. If all or any part of the Property is taken in condemnation proceedings instituted under power of eminent domain or is conveyed in lieu thereof under threat of condemnation, the money paid pursuant to such condemnation or conveyance in lieu thereof shall be applied to payment of the amounts payable by Purchaser under this contract, even if such amounts are not then due to be paid. Such amounts shall be applied first to unpaid accrued interest and next to the installments to be paid as provided in this contract in the inverse order of their maturity. Such payment shall not postpone the due date of the installments to be paid pursuant to this contract or change the amount of such installments. The balance, if any, shall be the property of Purchaser.

12. WASTE, REPAIR AND LIENS. Purchaser shall not remove or demolish any buildings, improvements or fixtures now or later located on or a part of the Property, nor shall Purchaser commit or allow waste of the Property. Purchaser shall maintain the Property in good condition and repair. Purchaser shall not create or permit to accrue liens or adverse claims against the Property which constitute a lien or claim against Seller's interest in the Property. Purchaser shall pay to Seller all amounts, costs and expenses, including reasonable attorneys' fees, incurred by Seller to remove any such liens or adverse claims.

13. DEED AND MORTGAGE REGISTRY TAXES. Seller shall, upon Purchaser's full performance of this contract, pay the deed tax due upon the recording or filing of the deed to be delivered by Seller to Purchaser. The mortgage registry tax due upon the recording or filing of this contract shall be paid by the party who records or files this contract; however, this provision shall not impair the right of Seller to collect from Purchaser the amount of such tax actually paid by Seller as provided in the applicable law governing default and service of notice of termination of this contract.

14. NOTICE OF ASSIGNMENT. If either Seller or Purchaser assigns their interest in the Property, a copy of such assignment shall promptly be furnished to the non-assigning party.

15. PROTECTION OF INTERESTS. If Purchaser fails to pay any sum of money required under the terms of this contract or fails to perform any of Purchaser's obligations as set forth in this contract, Seller may, at Seller's option, pay the same or cause the same to be performed, or both, and the amounts so paid by Seller and the cost of such performance shall be payable at once, with interest at the rate stated in paragraph 4 of this contract, as an additional amount due Seller under this contract.

If there now exists, or if Seller hereafter creates, suffers or permits to accrue, any mortgage, contract for deed, lien or encumbrance against the Property which is not herein expressly assumed by Purchaser, and provided Purchaser is not in default under this contract, Seller shall timely pay all amounts due thereon, and if Seller fails to do so, Purchaser may, at Purchaser's option, pay any such delinquent amounts and deduct the amounts paid from the installment(s) next coming due under this contract.

16. DEFAULT. The time of performance by Purchaser of the terms of this contract is an essential part of this contract. Should Purchaser fail to timely perform any of the terms of this contract, Seller may, at Seller's option, elect to declare this contract cancelled and terminated by notice to Purchaser in accordance with applicable law. All right, title and interest acquired under this contract by Purchaser shall then cease and terminate, and all improvements made upon the Property and all payments made by Purchaser pursuant to this contract shall belong to Seller as liquidated damages for breach of this contract. Neither the extension of the time for payment of any sum of money to be paid hereunder nor any waiver by Seller of Seller's rights to declare this contract forfeited by reason of any breach shall in any manner affect Seller's right to cancel this contract because of defaults subsequently occurring, and no extension of time shall be valid unless agreed to in writing. After service of notice of default and failure to cure such default within the period allowed by law, Purchaser shall, upon demand, surrender possession of the Property to Seller, but Purchaser shall be entitled to possession of the Property until the expiration of such period.

17. BINDING EFFECT. The terms of this contract shall run with the land and bind the parties hereto and their successors in interest.

18. HEADINGS. Headings of the paragraphs of this contract are for convenience only and do not define, limit or construe the contents of such paragraphs.

19. ASSESSMENTS BY OWNERS' ASSOCIATION. If the Property is subject to a recorded declaration providing for assessments to be levied against the Property by any owners' association, which assessments may become a lien against the Property if not paid, then:

    (a) Purchaser shall promptly pay, when due, all assessments imposed by the owners' association or other governing body as required by the provisions of the declaration or other related documents; and

    (b) So long as the owners' association maintains a master or blanket policy of insurance against fire, extended coverage perils and such other hazards and in such amounts as are required by this contract, then:

        (i) Purchaser's obligation in this contract to maintain hazard insurance coverage on the Property is satisfied; and

        (ii) The provisions in paragraph 8 of this contract regarding application of insurance proceeds shall be superceded by the provisions of the declaration or other related documents; and

(iii) In the event of a distribution of insurance proceeds in lieu of restoration or repair following an insured casualty loss to the Property, any such proceeds payable to Purchaser are hereby assigned and shall be paid to Seller for application to the sum secured by this contract, with the excess, if any, paid to Purchaser.

20. ADDITIONAL TERMS:

SELLER(S)   PURCHASER(S)

_____   _____

_____   _____

_____   _____

_____   _____

State of _____ } *ss.*

County of _____

The foregoing instrument was acknowledged before me this ____ day of _____ , 19___ ,
by _____ .

NOTARIAL STAMP OR SEAL (OR OTHER TITLE OR RANK)

_____
SIGNATURE OF NOTARY PUBLIC OR OTHER OFFICIAL

State of _____ } *ss.*

County of _____

The foregoing instrument was acknowledged before me this ____ day of _____ , 19___ ,
by _____ .

NOTARIAL STAMP OR SEAL (OR OTHER TITLE OR RANK)

_____
SIGNATURE OF NOTARY PUBLIC OR OTHER OFFICIAL

Tax Statements for the real property described in this instrument should be sent to:

THIS INSTRUMENT WAS DRAFTED BY (NAME AND ADDRESS):

FAILURE TO RECORD OR FILE THIS CONTRACT FOR DEED MAY GIVE OTHER PARTIES PRIORITY OVER PURCHASER'S INTEREST IN THE PROPERTY.

or spend it. Usually that seller is fairly well off financially and is in a position to carry the contract.

NEGOTIATE THE INTEREST

Most sellers like to get their price for the property. In this case, I like to negotiate the interest and the down payment, rather than the price. Let's take a case in point. A seller has a $100,000 property and he offers it for sale. He asks the $100,000 and wants $5,000 down with 11 percent interest on a 15-year contract. The monthly payment on this contract would be $1,022.67.

My theory is make a counteroffer on this kind of purchase: $100,000 for the property, 9 percent interest, and no down payment. The payment on this, as you can see, with less interest, is $1,004.52. If the seller won't negotiate without a down payment, offer the $5,000 and 9 percent interest. The payment then is $954.30 per month.

As you can see, negotiating the interest on a contract purchase can sometimes be a better bargaining chip than negotiating the actual price of the property—unless, of course, the price of the property is way out of line. Remember too, on a contract-for-deed purchase there are no closing costs, which amount to $3,000 in some mortgage loans. Points, fees, appraisals, etc. are also eliminated, thus giving the buyer some leeway with the price.

Here's another benefit of the contract for deed compared to the mortgage. Let's say the buyer gets into financial trouble and can't make a payment. By contacting the seller and holder of the contract, this problem usually can be worked out either by extending the payment or establishing smaller payments. The seller will try to negotiate something to save the contract and not have to take the property back. I doubt that this kind of thing can be worked out with a conventional bank loan.

I've been contacted by buyers of my contract for deeds and have negotiated terms to take care of their various temporary problems. I might add that during this time I've charged interest on the contract, and you can anticipate that this will happen. Often this solution can solve a problem that could otherwise become a disaster.

There's one more advantage of a contract for deed compared to the rigidness of a bank mortgage. Let's say the buyer has paid on a contract for deed for a number of years and there's a balance of $35,000 on the contract. The buyer often can negotiate a payoff on this contract for, let's say, $30,000 or $32,000. Discounting contract for deeds is a common occurrence. I'm not saying all contract holders will take this discount, but it's certainly something worth pursuing and is very probable.

This negotiated payoff can take place at a time of refinancing. If the buyer has paid off the contract, there's a chance the property has enough equity to qualify for a conventional loan.

Also, when buying property without a down payment, it's possible to negotiate a contract for deed with the seller for the down payment. Some sellers are more than happy to do this financing so they can close a sale. If you consider going this route, be sure to contact the bank before getting involved. Also, make certain there's enough cash flow to pay the contract payment and the mortgage payment.

BE WELL PREPARED

Once you have found a property, the next step is setting the plan in action. Of course, the first thing is agree with the seller on the price, down payment, interest, length of contract, and any other terms.

Then provide a good financial report to the seller to establish credibility. After all, he's turning his property over to you and has a right to know if he's going to get paid. You can bet the seller isn't going to be interested in dealing with an unreliable buyer—one who mismanages property and one who is financially irresponsible.

It's not only good to have a well-prepared financial statement for the seller to establish this credibility, but it serves as a reference for future purchases.

BUYER PROTECTION OF A CONTRACT FOR DEED

The seller obviously needs protection, but it's equally important for the buyer to have the same protection. You'll see why as we go along.

Check out the seller. Go to your credit bureau and buy a report. Know who you're dealing with.

One reason you want to know the seller is that he—after, before, or during the time of the contract-for-deed sale—can carry a mortgage on the property. If the payments on the mortgage are not paid as agreed, the holder of the mortgage can foreclose on the property and they have no responsibility to the contract-for-deed buyer. That means you could pay on a contract for deed for five years and then find out the bank is taking the property back, leaving you high and dry with no chance whatsoever to recover all the payments you have made.

There are several ways for you, the buyer, to protect yourself in this kind of transaction. First, and foremost of course, is *know* the seller. Second, have written into the contract for deed that the mortgage payments will be made directly to the mortgage holder by the contract buyer. Third, have the mortgage holder notify the contract buyer whenever a payment is missed.

KEEP PRECISE RECORDS

If and when you buy real estate on a contract for deed, of course, you will have monthly payments. Usually these contract for deeds are for many years and, during that period of time, it's easy for the records to get mixed up. To avoid any confusion or conflict, when you are making out the check each and every month, include all information right on the check.

Let me give you an example of what I mean. Let's say it's a $40,000, 9 percent, 10-year contract for deed. The payment on this contract is $500.28. On the 30th payment, the interest is $246.82, the principal is $253.46, and the balance is $32,656.03. This is the information you need to keep on record. Do it each month right on the check. In this way, there's no way the contract holder can come back and tell you there's a different balance or that you missed a payment.

FORECLOSURE TIME AND CONDITIONS

As a buyer on a contract for deed, you need to have a complete understanding of the terms. On most contract for deeds, if a payment is in default for as little as 30 days, the holder of that contract can take possession and void the contract. Here's what could happen. The buyer could pay on this contract for 5 or 10 years then find it difficult to make the payments for one reason or another. At that point the seller could take back the property and keep all the money that had been paid during that 5 or 10 years. Not only would you lose the equity, but also the hard work and the appreciation you had built up in the property.

If this should happen, however, I have a feeling that a court would rule in favor of the buyer, and he should be able to recover some of this equity. Let's put it this way; if I've paid for 10 years and built up this equity, I'm going to fight to get at least part of it, and I'd take my case to court to recover as much as possible.

Here's another concern for the contract-for-deed buyer. If the holder of the contract for deed—the seller—files bankruptcy, the bankruptcy attorney can claim the property. The equity in that property becomes an asset of the bankruptcy. That means if you've paid off $5,000 in equity, it is no longer yours. In order to save the property, you might have to come up with another $5,000 or just give the property back to the seller. In addition, all the rents accumulated during the period of the bankruptcy become assets of the bankruptcy. They can collect the rent and not make the payments on the contract for deed.

Very little protection exists in a case like this, other than to *know* the seller and holder of your contract for deed. Also, have an attorney present when transacting the deal.

Also, no loan agency or bank will give you a mortgage on a property you purchased by contract for deed. The title must be clear of the contract for deed first.

When purchasing any property, whether it's a contract for deed or any other kind of purchase, be sure to have your attorney check for any mortgages on the property and judgments against the individual. Your attorney should advise you that these judgments must be settled before clear title is issued on the property.

While I am on the subject of attorneys, make sure your attorney knows real estate. Make sure that your deed and purchase agreement contains a full legal description of the property. If it doesn't, it can become costly and troublesome to clear up the title.

THE CONTRACT FOR DEED WITH A BALLOON PAYMENT

Usually, sellers of property on a contract for deed want their money as quickly as possible. Most of the time the contract seller wants a five-year payoff, or what is known as a *balloon payment*. This balloon payment is great for the seller, but not so good for the buyer. The reason why it isn't very good for the buyer is that in five years all that he has paid is interest on the loan; he has very little equity.

Here's an example of what this kind of contract means. I sold a property on a contract for deed, at a price of $31,701, amortized over 25 years, at 9½ percent interest with a balloon payment in five years. The buyer is paying $295.50 per month, or a total of $17,700 in five years. However, only $3,332 of that $17,700 is equity, which means the buyer will have to come up with $28,369 at the end of five years.

As you can see, the balloon payment deal isn't all that great for the buyer. The alternative is to ask for a 10-year balloon or, if the seller insists on 5 years, find a way to make a big enough payment so that there's equity built up in that 5-year period. After all, the main reason anyone is in the real estate business is to gain equity.

This information pretty much covers the basics of the contract for deed. The main thing is to have an understanding of how it works.

Even though there are some negative features of the contract for deed, I'm totally convinced it's a great way to buy investment property. For some of us, it's the only way.

I can only add this bit of advice. When entering into a contract-for-deed purchase, be sure you know who you're dealing with, know what you're doing, have it in writing, and have good legal advice.

THE EARNEST MONEY CONTRACT

Basically, the contract for sale, purchase agreement, and earnest money contract are one and the same agreement. It simply means there's a buyer and a seller, and the two agree with this document to buy and sell a piece of real estate. Typical contracts are shown in Figs. 7-2 and 7-3.

The main point to consider when transacting a purchase agreement is to get everything in writing. Following is a list of important things you should not overlook when you are drawing up the contract:

- A complete description of the property
- A statement of personal property
- The purchase price
- Encumbrances and mortgages against the property
- Property restrictions
- Assessments

When negotiating a purchase agreement, make sure there's an understanding right from the start who pays what taxes. Here's the way I work it. The owner of the property pays all taxes due for the time of possession. The buyer then pays the taxes effective the day he takes over the property.

Also, when drawing up a contract for sale for rental property, stipulate who collects the rents between the time the contract is being drawn up and the completion date. Also spell out if there's interest due, and who pays for the insurance during this time.

Be concerned who pays for the following during the transition period:

- Utilities
- Water
- Sewer tax
- Assessments

In the contract, make sure it's understood who assumes any existing mortgage payments. Once again, have legal representation.

THE QUIT CLAIM DEED

The *quit claim deed* is a fairly simple deed, in which the seller gives up his or her interest in the property. Of course, there could be other interested parties to that real estate. Have legal representation when dealing with quit claim deeds. Figure 7-4 shows a typical Quit Claim Deed.

THE GENERAL WARRANTY DEED

Several different warranty deeds can be used. Figure 7-5 shows an individual to individual warranty deed. As you transact real estate, your legal representative will make certain the proper deed is completed.

PURCHASE AGREEMENT

.... **Minn.,** ...., 19.........

RECEIVED OF ....

the sum of .... ($...................) DOLLARS

....**as** earnest money and in part payment for the purchase of property at
(Check, Cash, to be deposited upon acceptance, or Note — State Which)

.... situated in the

County of ...., State of .... and legally described as follows, to-wit:

including all garden bulbs, plants, shrubs and trees, all storm sash, storm doors, detachable vestibules, screens, awnings, window shades, blinds (including venetian blinds), curtain rods, traverse rods, drapery rods, lighting fixtures and bulbs, plumbing fixtures, hot water tanks and heating plant (with any burners, tanks, stokers and other equipment used in connection therewith), water softener and liquid gas tank and controls (if the property of seller), sump pump, television antenna, incinerator, built-in dishwasher, garbage disposal, ovens, cook top stoves and central air conditioning equipment, if any, used and located on said premises and including also the following personal property:

all of which property the undersigned has this day sold to the buyer for the sum of:

.... ($...................) DOLLARS,

which the buyer agrees to pay in the following manner:

Earnest money herein paid $.................... and $...................., cash, on ...., the date of closing.

Subject to performance by the buyer the seller agrees to execute and deliver a .... Warranty Deed
(to be joined in by spouse, if any) conveying marketable title to said premises subject only to the following exceptions:
(a) Building and zoning laws, ordinances, State and Federal regulations.
(b) Restrictions relating to use or improvement of premises without effective forfeiture provision.
(c) Reservation of any minerals or mineral rights to the State of Minnesota.
(d) Utility and drainage easements which do not interfere with present improvements.
(e) Rights of tenants as follows: (unless specified, not subject to tenancies)
  The buyer shall pay the real estate taxes due in the year 19 .... and any unpaid installments of special assessments payable therewith and thereafter. Seller warrants that real estate taxes due in the year 19 ......will be .... homestead classification
(full, partial or non-homestead — state which)
  Neither the seller nor the seller's agent make any representation or warranty whatsoever concerning the amount of real estate taxes which shall be assessed against the property subsequent to the date of purchase.
  Seller covenants that buildings, if any, are entirely within the boundary lines of the property and agrees to remove all personal property not included herein and all debris from the premises prior to possession date. SELLER WARRANTS ALL APPLIANCES, HEATING, AIR CONDITIONING, WIRING AND PLUMBING USED AND LOCATED ON SAID PREMISES ARE IN PROPER WORKING ORDER AT DATE OF CLOSING.
  The seller further agrees to deliver possession not later than .... provided that all conditions of this agreement have been complied with. Unless otherwise specified this sale shall be closed on or before 60 days from the date hereof.
  In the event this property is destroyed or substantially damaged by fire or any other cause before the closing date, this agreement shall become null and void, at the purchaser's option, and all monies paid hereunder shall be refunded to him.
  The buyer and seller also mutually agree that pro rata adjustments of rents, interest, insurance and city water, and, in the case of income property, current operating expenses, shall be made as of ....
  The seller shall, within a reasonable time after approval of this agreement, furnish an abstract of title, or a Registered Property Abstract certified to date to include proper searches covering bankruptcies, and State and Federal judgments and liens. The buyer shall be allowed 10 days after receipt thereof for examination of said title and the making of any objections thereto, said objections to be made in writing or deemed to be waived. If any objections are so made the seller shall be allowed 120 days to make such title marketable. Pending correction of title the payments hereunder required shall be postponed, but upon correction of title and within 10 days after written notice to the buyer, the parties shall perform this agreement according to its terms.
  If said title is not marketable and is not made so within 120 days from the date of written objections thereto as above provided, this agreement shall be null and void, at option of the buyer, and neither principal shall be liable for damages hereunder to the other principal. All money theretofore paid by the buyer shall be refunded. If the title to said property be found marketable or be so made within said time, and said buyer shall default in any of the agreements and continue in default for a period of 10 days, then and in that case the seller may terminate this contract and on such termination all the payments made upon this contract shall be retained by said seller and said agent, as their respective interests may appear, as liquidated damages, time being of the essence hereof. This provision shall not deprive either party of the right of enforcing the specific performance of this contract provided such contract shall not be terminated as aforesaid, and provided action to enforce such specific performance shall be commenced within six months after such right of action shall arise.
  It is understood and agreed that this sale is made subject to the approval by the owner of said premises in writing and that the undersigned agent is in no manner liable or responsible on account of this agreement, except to return or account for the earnest money paid under this contract.

The delivery of all papers and monies shall be made at the office of: ....

....

I, the undersigned, owner of the above land, do hereby approve the above agreement and the sale thereby made.

By .... Agent

I hereby agree to purchase the said property for the price and upon the terms above mentioned, and subject to all conditions herein expressed.

.... (SEAL)
Seller

.... (SEAL)
Buyer

.... (SEAL)
Seller

.... (SEAL)
Buyer

Fig. 7-2. A purchase agreement.

EARNEST MONEY CONTRACT OF SALE. (WITHOUT AGENT)

....19...........

RECEIVED OF ....

.... Dollars ($..................................)

as Earnest Money, and in part payment for the purchase of the following described property situated

in the County of ....and State of .... viz:

which .... have this day sold and agreed to convey to said ....

.... for the

sum of .... Dollars ($..................................)
on terms as follows, viz:

.... Dollars ($................................),
in hand paid as above, and

payable on or before the dates as named above, or as soon thereafter as a Warranty Deed conveying a
good title to said land is tendered, time being considered of the essence of this Contract.
It is understood that complete abstract of title continued to date is to be furnished to purchaser......
at the expense of vendor......, after which..........................days is to be allowed purchaser...... for examination of title and report.
Such purchaser agree to pay all taxes or assessments, or installments thereof, that may hereafter become payable on said property from date hereof, including unpaid installments of special assessments heretofore levied on
said property.

And it is agreed that if the title to said premises is not good and cannot be made good within
.... days from date hereof, this agreement shall be void, and the above earnest money refunded. But if the title to said premises is now good, in the name of the vendor......, or is made good
in him within .... days, and said purchaser...... refuses to accept the same, said above mentioned earnest money shall be forfeited to the undersigned owner ....

But it is agreed and understood by all parties to this agreement that said forfeiture shall in no
way affect the right of either party to enforce the specific performance of this Contract.

..........................hereby agree to purchase the said property for the price and upon the terms above
mentioned, and also agree to the conditions of forfeiture and all other conditions therein expressed.

....

....

..........................the undersigned, owner...... of the above described land, do hereby agree to sell the said
property for the price and upon the terms above mentioned.

....

....

Fig. 7-3. An Earnest Money Contract for Sale.

State of .... }
County of .... } ss.
....

On this .... day of .... A. D. 19 ...., before me,
.... a .... within and for said
County and State, personally appeared ....

.... to me known to be the same person
described in and who executed the foregoing instrument, and acknowledged that   he   executed
the same as .... free act and deed.

....

....

Earnest Money Contract

–QUIT CLAIM DEED

Individual (s) to Individual (s)

No delinquent taxes and transfer entered; Certificate
of Real Estate Value (   ) filed (   ) not required
Certificate of Real Estate Value No._____
_____ , 19_____

_____
                                        County Auditor

by_____
                                              Deputy

STATE DEED TAX DUE HEREON: $ _____

Date: _____ , 19 ____

(reserved for recording data)

FOR VALUABLE CONSIDERATION, _____
_____ , Grantor (s),
                                        (marital status)

hereby convey (s) and quitclaim (s) to _____
_____ , Grantee (s),

real property in _____ County, _____ , described as follows:

(if more space is needed, continue on back)
together with all hereditaments and appurtenances belonging thereto.

Affix Deed Tax Stamp Here

_____

_____

_____

STATE OF _____ }
                                                 } ss.
COUNTY OF _____ }

_____

The foregoing instrument was acknowledged before me this_____day of_____ , 19____,
by _____
_____ , Grantor (s).

NOTARIAL STAMP OR SEAL (OR OTHER TITLE OR RANK)

_____
SIGNATURE OF PERSON TAKING ACKNOWLEDGMENT

Tax Statements for the real property described in this instrument should
be sent to (Include name and address of Grantee):

THIS INSTRUMENT WAS DRAFTED BY (NAME AND ADDRESS):

Fig. 7-4. A quit claim deed.

WARRANTY DEED

Individual (s) to Individual (s)

No delinquent taxes and transfer entered; Certificate of Real Estate Value (   ) filed (   ) not required
Certificate of Real Estate Value No._____
_____ , 19 _____

_____
County Auditor

by _____
Deputy

STATE DEED TAX DUE HEREON: $ _____

Date: _____ , 19 _____

(reserved for recording data)

FOR VALUABLE CONSIDERATION, _____
_____ , Grantor (s),
(marital status)

hereby convey (s) and warrant (s) to _____
_____ , Grantee (s),
real property in _____ County,   , described as follows:

(if more space is needed, continue on back)

together with all hereditaments and appurtenances belonging thereto, subject to the following exceptions:

Affix Deed Tax Stamp Here

_____

_____

_____

_____

STATE OF

COUNTY OF _____ } ss.

_____

The foregoing instrument was acknowledged before me this _____ day of _____ , 19____,
by _____
_____ , Grantor (s).

NOTARIAL STAMP OR SEAL (OR OTHER TITLE OR RANK)

_____
SIGNATURE OF PERSON TAKING ACKNOWLEDGMENT

Tax Statements for the real property described in this instrument should be sent to (Include name and address of Grantee):

THIS INSTRUMENT WAS DRAFTED BY (NAME AND ADDRESS):

Fig. 7-5. A warranty deed.

In general, the warranty deed is the most secure. It means that the owner is guaranteeing the title from defects and previous owners. As with anything else, however, there can be exceptions. Therefore, as with all other real estate transactions, make sure you have legal advice in getting a clear title.

THE RIGHT TO RESCIND

The consumer Credit Protection Act gives the buyer the right to rescind the purchase up to midnight of the third business day following the transaction date. This right gives the buyer time to think it over and back out if he desires.

GETTING CLEAR TITLE

Getting clear title is something that can't be overlooked. Not getting it done right the first time can be costly and time-consuming.Therefore, get an attorney who knows titles. Here's why.

I know a case where an individual bought a piece of property from an estate. The title of the property had been transacted several times from the time the original owners had sold it out of the estate. However, it was found out that no one had transferred the grandchildren's interest in this title. That meant it was necessary to go back to these interested parties and get a deed signed. Fortunately, they were cooperative and eventually the title was cleared, but it could have been costly.

A lot of stories could be told about titles. As an example, I knew of one title that couldn't be transacted until they got 42 different parties to sign off interest on the property. It was, again, one of those estates that had never been cleared.

The point is, have good representation to clear that title. Don't try to make up deeds, clear titles, or read abstracts on your own. As all the work is transacted, there are costs. Know who pays for what.

READING THE ABSTRACT

In all likelihood you've seen an abstract (Fig. 7-6). *Reading the abstract* means getting a title opinion. This opinion is given by an attorney or abstract company. It's the buyer's responsibility to make sure it's updated; however, it's usually the seller's obligation to pay the necessary fees. You should know who will pay the fees ahead of time.

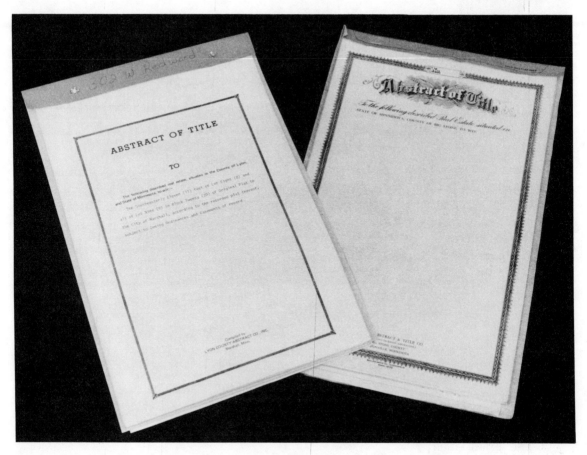

Fig. 7-6. Keep all abstracts in a safe place. Replacement cost can be several hundred dollars.

DEED TAX

One last item on deeds; most states have a deed tax that must be paid at the time of registering the mortgage and deed. Have in writing who pays this tax.

HIRING AN APPRAISER

An appraiser charges about $100 for his services. An independent appraiser will usually give the fair and marketable value of the property. This appraisal is usually based on the valuation of other similar properties, along with other relevant information regarding the property.

It's not necessary to have an appraisal done if you feel comfortable with the price, but if you're not quite sure, it might be a good investment. It's optional, other than when taking out a loan from the FHA or a bank. These institutions demand an appraised valuation. At any rate, it might contribute to your peace of mind to have it done.

THE REAL ESTATE CONTRACT

If you have a contract with a real estate agent, make sure the contract clearly states who pays what. This contract sometimes can and will go along with the Purchase Agreement, but some agents have their own contract.

Following are some expenses incurred that should be spelled out before everything is completed:

- Lender inspection fee
- Advance commitment fee
- Loan processing fee
- FHA mortgage fund fee
- Prepaid interest
- Mortgage insurance reserve
- Credit report fee
- Settlement escrow fee
- Document preparation
- Attorney fee
- Recording fee
- State stamps
- Pest inspection
- Mortgage insurance premium
- Appraisal report fee
- Appraiser inspection fee
- Title examination
- Notary fee
- Title insurance fee
- State tax
- Survey

Obviously, all these charges aren't made on all real estate, and most of them aren't made on a contract-for-deed sale. However, a lot of them are a part of real estate sales. It's best to have some awareness of them.

8

The New Tax Laws

I WAS ASKED ONCE, "IF YOU COULD GIVE ONLY ONE REASON AND ONE reason alone why anyone should buy real estate, what would it be?" Without hesitation I was able to answer that question easily, and said, the tax benefits!

That's it, pure and simple. The tax loophole, tax break, tax incentive, tax write-off, or whatever you want to call it, is simply a legal and government-sanctioned method to eliminate the payment of taxes.

The great part of the real estate tax write-off is that it not only applies to the actual property itself, but can be charged back to the investor's individual income as a deduction. That means if there are losses in your real estate business and the losses are coming from depreciation, insurance, cost of operations, real estate taxes, maintenance and upkeep, and improvements, they can be charged as a loss on personal income. Everyone, and I mean *everyone*, in the real estate business knows about this tax break and considers it to be one of the best incentives for buying investment property.

A TAX WRITE-OFF MEANS PROFITS AND SAVINGS

A tax write-off means money in the bank. Tax write-off is such an integral part of the real estate business; no part of it should be overlooked. In the following paragraphs, we're going to look at this tax advantage in depth.

A lot of people don't understand that a tax is profit because they can't really see the money; it's often subdued and hidden. It's not like having cash that we can deposit in the bank. Believe me, though, it's there. It took me several years to fully understand what affect it had on my overall income tax, but once the accountant showed me how much money I *didn't* have to pay the government, then I knew, and you will, too.

Let's take a sharper look at all the benefits.

TAX DEPRECIATION: MONEY IN THE BANK

Depreciation is the créme de la créme. It's a clear-cut gift to the investor. Let's look at a hypothetical investment. Our investor owns a $100,000 investment property with a depreciation period of 27.5 years. The investor pays 28 percent income tax on his total income. These figures mean that each year for 27.5 years, our investor will have a $1,018.18 tax deduction. This deduction can carry over to his personal income tax filing.

Depreciation is great, but it's not the only benefit. Others exist, and for this reason, new laws or old, no one should be discouraged from buying, owning, and investing in property.

In fact, the small investor, like you and me, should continue doing just what he's been doing—buying real estate. If you haven't started, there's no reason to hesitate.

––––––––––––

For the small investor, the future in real estate is indeed bright. There's always going to be a need for housing, regardless of the Internal Revenue Service (IRS) tax laws. This fact means housing is a growing business.

––––––––––––

We've been given a distorted view about the new tax laws. As you listen to some of the news stories, it almost sounds like everything is gone.

As a matter of fact, I've been asked, "What are you going to do now that you've lost all the tax benefits of owning investment real estate?" The answer to that is simple. I haven't lost the benefits; they are very much there and I intend to continue buying. Some changes have been enacted, but nothing so radical that would make real estate anything but a positive investment.

The majority of investors I know are in the real estate business for the long haul and to make money, not just for the tax benefits. With this combination, you simply can't miss. All investors know that real estate represents a business in which you can use other people's money—the banks and tenants—to develop a great savings and build a secure future.

They also know that their income and net worth can be increased through appreciation and equity. Most importantly, they all expect to make money in real estate under the new tax laws.

THE MEANING OF THE NEW REAL ESTATE TAX LAWS

Let's get the story straight. What do the new laws mean, and how do they affect each of us? Let's take one at a time.

Depreciation. As the new law is written, all properties owned up to and through the year 1986 can continue using the old depreciation schedules, which is for a period of 19 years.

As I've mentioned, depreciation is such an integral noncash tax deduction that it has a strong impact on our investment. *Depreciation* is the wear and tear of the property. Money is not involved. In fact, it's more like a gift. The ironical part of depreciation is that while we're using depreciation on our tax write-off and making money, in all likelihood, the property is appreciating—actually increasing in value.

Under the new law, all rental investment properties purchased after December 31, 1986, must be depreciated over 27.5 years, rather than 19 years.

Depreciation over 27.5 years isn't all that bad, especially for the small investors who are in for the long haul. The way I figure it, many of the large investors will discontinue building the large apartment complexes. This decrease in construction obviously is going to increase the demand for existing apartments, which in turn will increase rents. Another benefit for the small investor is the new clause in the tax law, which prohibits a passive owner from benefiting from the tax deductions. This clause means that any individual or business that does not materially participate in the property can't use it for tax write-offs. Again, the wealthy investor might not look so grandly at real estate as an investment and, it will further mean that those investors who are in the business are going to have to make the property *cash flow*; that is make a profit.

Real estate investing is a form of forced savings. We're forced to save other people's money: the banks', the tenants', and the government's.

Professional Property Management. Another part of the new passive clause in the law states that any owner who hires a professional property management firm can no longer take the deduction from personal income. Again, this doesn't really affect the small investor.

Investment Losses. Here's another new tax law. If the investor earns less than $100,000 yearly, adjusted gross income, that investor can deduct up to $25,000 of annual losses from the properties. Although this law doesn't affect most of us, you should remember that any unused losses can be carried forward to future tax years or can become a deduction at the time the property is sold.

I've briefly covered the changes that involve the small real estate investor. However, if you're not sure about these laws, you should contact an accountant and go over the laws with him. At the same time, have him analyze what affect real estate investment can have on your overall income tax.

AN HONEST TAX PLAN IS THE BEST PLAN

To stress the importance of taking advantage of all the tax benefits of real estate investing, here are some theories I advocate:

- Pay every penny of personal and investment income tax due.
- Operate the real estate business with complete and total honesty.
- Take every conceivable deduction the law allows.

The reason I say you should pay every penny of personal and investment income tax due is because there's no sense looking for trouble. The last thing you want to deal with is an IRS audit.

I also state that you should operate the real estate business with complete and total honesty. Plenty of benefits are available in the real estate business, so there's no reason to be dishonest.

Also, I say take every conceivable deduction the law allows because that's precisely what I mean. There's a lot more to say about this theory.

I'll start by telling you that every time you turn around in your real estate business and you use shoe leather doing it, take the shoe repairman's bill as a deduction. Don't let a single penny slip through the cracks because, if you do, it's money out of your pocket—it's profit lost.

You must count the pennies, and the dollars will add up. As can be seen in Fig. 8-1, I've made a list of deductions so none are overlooked. I didn't put this list in just to fill space, but to remind you that nothing should be overlooked. Every item, and I've probably missed some, is used in one way or another in the investment business. Use all of them. Deduct any product and/or service if it applies to the investment property.

Let's go back a little to being honest and not cheating. Don't ask for trouble. For instance, some things are not deductible. It would be difficult to justify buying 12 boxes of shot-gun shells in the fall of the year and charging this expenditure to the security of your property. If, how-

TOOLS	LAWNMOWERS	SCREWS, NUTS, BOLTS
FLASHLIGHT	CLEANING MATERIALS	SOAP
DRAINO	BROOMS, BRUSHES	CAR
GAS AND OIL	CAR EXPENSE	CAR REPAIR
TRANSPORTATION	REAL ESTATE TRIPS	PENS, PENCILS
TYPEWRITER	TYPEWRITER RIBBONS	MACHINE REPAIR
BOOKS	SEMINARS	TELEPHONE
NEWSPAPERS	POSTAGE	INSURANCE
HEAT	LIGHTS	INTEREST
PAYROLL TAXES	SOCIAL SECURITY	TAXES
CAPITAL INVESTMENT	LEGAL FEES	ACCOUNTING
FEES	PROMOTIONS	ENTERTAINMENT
MEETINGS	CONVENTIONS	ADVERTISING
MEALS	DONATIONS	REPAIR
UTILITIES	DEPRECIATION	SPECIAL CLOTHING
SALARIES		

Fig. 8-1. Potential income tax deductions.

ever, you legitimately attend a real estate seminar in Tahiti, this trip, and the expenses, can be charged to your real estate investment.

If you're self-employed in the real estate business and have an office in your home, part of your home expenses can be deducted. On the other hand, I know an individual investor who put new carpeting in his home, did other repairs, and charged all these expenditures against the investment property. That is not acceptable to the IRS. But, you know, I'll bet that Mr. Big Investor, who owns all kinds of property, uses employees to care for his personal and recreational homes, which probably includes painting and repairing and upkeep.

I also wonder, if Joe Plumber comes into one of these homes to fix a leaky faucet or the painter does work in a personal home, that Mr. Big gets out his personal checkbook and writes out a personal check for this work.

THE FINANCIAL BENEFITS OF REPAIR VS. IMPROVEMENTS

It's important to understand the difference between a *repair* and an *improvement*. A repair is charged off as an expense. Improvements are capital investments and are deducted over a five-year period.

This difference is important because of the difference in the tax deduction. To better understand, let's see how they differ.

First, here's what the IRS says about repairs and improvements.

• You may deduct the cost of repairs that you make to your rental property. You may not deduct the cost of improvements. You recover these costs by taking depreciation.

• A repair keeps your property in good operating condition. It does not materially add to the value of the property or substantially prolong its life.

• An improvement adds to the value of the property, prolongs its useful life, or adapts it to new uses.

To be more specific, here's how it works. If there's a $200 repair, you get a $56 tax deduction. However, if it's an improvement, it represents a deduction of $11.20 per year for five years.

For the most part, the small investor is dealing with older properties that are in constant need of repair. For instance, fixing a leaky roof constitutes a repair, and this means if you put on a new roof, it was put on to repair the leak. The new roof doesn't substantially add to the value of the property; therefore the roof is considered to be a repair.

If the furnace breaks down in the middle of winter and a new one must be installed, it can be construed as a repair. You might ask, "What if I get audited?" Then I say, argue your case.

9

Enhancing Profits through Financial Concerns

I'D LIKE TO TELL YOU HOW TO OPERATE A REAL ESTATE BUSINESS, OR any other business for that matter, without bookkeeping, payroll, income tax reports, and all the other paperwork that goes along with the operation. As we all know, however, that's impossible. The next best thing is to find a way to keep the paperwork as simple and uncomplicated as possible. Let's start with bookkeeping.

HIRING A BOOKKEEPER

Be assured that if you contact an accountant or Certified Public Accountant (CPA), you're going to end up with an elaborate double-entry bookkeeping system. It's possible the system will be something you might not understand and one that's going to be costly. Don't be bamboozled into thinking you need a high-priced and time-consuming bookkeeping system.

To avoid costly accounting here's what I've done and it's worked for years. I set up a simple, inexpensive plan; one that I personally can work.

I simply use my checkbook. I have a 9½-×-12-inch, three-ring checkbook. Each page consists of three checks. Each time I pay a bill, I enter the transaction on the stub, showing the reason for the check and location of the property. At the end of the year, I simply add up the expenses from the stubs. I also staple the receipts right to the stub; thus I have a complete record of the transaction. I also record on the check stub the rental income. I do keep a monthly ledger of the tenant's rents in addition. Basically, however, this is my bookkeeping system and it's never failed me.

Keep the accounting of your business comparatively easy so you can devote more time to the profitable ventures—like looking for ways to cut costs, finding new properties to buy, and actually caring for the property you own.

Recognize and use your own creative skills. We all have them. Build your own program, whether it's bookkeeping, managing, or buying real estate. A positive, creative mind can greatly influence your success.

Keep Good Financial Records

Although I advocate keeping simple records, it's important that you keep good, understandable records. You need them for your own financial report, for your tax records, and for the possibility of an IRS audit.

I believe an audit is a fairly remote possibility for the small investor. If you follow the advice as given in Chapter 8 about being totally honest there's no reason to fear an audit.

I have to admit, I was audited once, a number of years ago. The IRS found nothing at fault and I'm convinced the reason was the fact that I had good, clear, and precise records.

I found the IRS is concerned about two items in an audit, other than honesty. One is that you keep receipts proving the respective expenditures. The other is the price you paid for the property. This price, of course, determines your depreciation, which, as I said before, is an important part of the real estate investment business. The IRS knows this, too.

If you don't keep good records and are audited, it can be very costly. You should never take this chance.

Keep Solid Proof of any Questionable Expenditure

As we all know, in any business there are perquisites, or "perks". Perks are looked at by the IRS with some mistrust.

Here's an example of what I mean. I have a good friend in the real estate business who likes to travel. Whenever he can, he'll attend real estate seminars in Acapulco, Hawaii, St. Thomas Island, or any other exotic place—especially in the winter since he's a midwesterner.

He has every right in the world to attend these meetings and every right to charge the expenses to the real estate investment business. If you find yourself in need of such a conference, by all means go.

If your spouse is an officer or coowner of your real estate business, and he/she should be, then he/she also has a right to attend these meetings. His/her expenses should also be charged to the real estate business.

I've told you that you can go. I've also told you that you can charge the expenses of this trip to your real estate business. I also want to tell you that the IRS has some reservations about perks and these kinds of trips. Since this is the case, here are some tips to follow.

When attending these meetings, keep an accurate and precise diary of events, which should include your complete daily activities, the meetings attended, the subject of the meetings, the names of the speakers, and a precise record of the expenses incurred each day, with receipts.

If, by chance, the IRS audits your records, you'll have positive proof of the deductions; deductions, I might add, that are justified and correct. It's a legitimate part of your business, so take them.

HOW TO DEAL WITH THE BUSINESS PAYROLL

If you hire people and put them on a payroll you will have considerable expenses, such as social security, unemployment insurance, and the cost of maintaining the income tax records.

In the small real estate business, there's no need to hire people as employees. It's best to hire individuals as contractors and have an understanding with them that they are not working on an hourly basis, but on a contract basis—per job. If necessary, have the agreement in writing. As you learn the business, you'll find there are a number of people out there who are willing to work part time, including retired carpenters, plumbers, painters, etc.

This is one of those cost-cutting ideas you can use as a shrewd investor.

Tenants Make Good Workers for Your Real Estate

Tenants are not only qualified in most cases, but eager to do a lot of the work in their own apartments. I've used them for painting, cleaning, fixing, and repairing, whatever and wherever.

Good, qualified tenants can make good property managers. They can clean halls, show apartments to new tenants, and make sure everything is in order and operating smoothly. Again, avoid the payroll by giving these tenants a deduction in their rents.

Consider the Family Payroll for Your Property

I've given you a lot of advice about avoiding a payroll. The next thing I'm going to talk about will totally conflict with this advice. That is, that the family payroll is a good real estate investment. Let me explain.

No matter if you own 1 unit or 100 units, if you have qualified family members—school-aged children who want to work—use them in the business. It's an excellent opportunity for them to earn college education money with pretaxed dollars. Obviously, they have to pay income tax on their income, but it is taken out of your income before it is taxed at a higher rate.

Family members can paint, fix, clean, mow lawns, or do any of the work around investment properties. If they're away at college, have them work on weekends, holidays, and vacations.

Not only is this a good money-maker for your family and business, but your children can receive an invaluable real estate education. I've even used my children as apartment managers and put them in decision-making positions. This experience has enhanced their real estate skills and, sometime in the future, this experience can, and will, pay off, either in the job market or in individual investments. It's a great learning experience for them.

BEAN COUNTERS CAN WRING OUT EXTRA PROFIT

Bean counters are the shrewd business managers who know how to squeeze out profits. They don't let anything financial slip through the cracks. Bean counters make sure you're not paying $119 for something that costs $99. They are competent financial and fiscal managers and know how to cut costs, scrutinize expenses, and make sure a dollar spent gets a dollar returned.

Operating as a bean counter means shopping for all bargains. It means chiseling the price whenever and wherever you can. This chiseling applies to materials and equipment, as well as to real estate itself.

The epitome of the bean counters was a guy named Ben Franklin, who said, "A penny saved is a penny earned." Watching the expenses on small items pays off handsomely in the profit picture.

"BEAN COUNT" YOUR INSURANCE COSTS

Insurance is a highly competitive business. Many agents would like to write your business. Shop around, contact several agents, and negotiate prices. There's no reason to take the first bid, unless it's the best.

Also, check the deductible clause of your insurance policies. I was able to save a 20 percent premium cost by increasing the deductible from $100 to $500.

Most small real estate investors, like myself, fix wind-torn doors or broken windows, and usually don't file the small claims. The insurance is needed for major losses.

Ask for Monthly Premium Payments

Monthly insurance payments don't save money, but can certainly help the cash flow. Ask your agent to carry your premium account on a 30-day-monthly pay plan. That way, there's no large premium due. However, be sure your agent will carry this type of payment without an interest charge.

Incidentally, it's a good idea to have only one agent. He's apt to treat and regard your business more fairly and have more concern about costs.

Understand and Know Your Insurance Coverage

Scrutinize your insurance policy. Go over it with your agent so you know what coverage the policy provides. Following are some examples of insurance covering rental property.

If you own a single-family rental unit or a duplex, you can add these properties onto your homeowner's policy for liability. You do, however, need a policy for each property to cover fire and extended coverage.

There's a policy called Special Multi-Peril Insurance, which covers more than two units. Also, there's a policy called Owners, Landlords and Tenants Liability.

Following is a list of concerns that you should include in whatever insurance you have:

- Fire
- Lightning
- Windstorm or hail
- Explosion
- Riot
- Vehicle
- Vandalism
- Theft
- Smoke from faulty operation of heating or cooking
- Damage from steam or hot water
- Accidental leakage from plumbing, heating, appliances
- Freezing of plumbing, heating and air conditioning
- Damage to electrical appliances
- Falling objects
- Snow, ice, sleet, collapse of building
- Glass breakage
- Physical loss to building
- Liability, medical and accidental death

Endorsements are available for most policies and can cover personal liability, and loss of income. Again, be sure you consult with your agent to make sure you have adequate coverage.

How to Keep from Going Broke With Status Symbols

Years ago, when I was a status seeker—and I was one—I wish someone would have hit me over the head and wakened me to the futility of buying all kinds of status symbols, especially new cars.

If I had bought real estate instead of cars, I'd be a millionaire many times over. But no, I got caught in the new car trap and bought cars and cars and cars—ad infinitum.

The remarkable thing is, one year one car wasn't enough. First I bought a new Buick Special. Ten months later, that same year, I had to have a 1953 Buick Roadmaster—the best and most expensive. That year I spent enough hard-earned money to make a down payment on a duplex, four-plex, or any other investment property. I ended up with a multitude of monthly payments and a worn-out car. The worst part of it is, the car dealer got my money and bought real estate. Today he's wealthy.

New, flashy, expensive cars, like other insignificant status symbols, are a game people play. If you play right along with them, it's going to cost and probably keep you comparatively broke. I know this, these *things* will keep you working hard all your life, and I can guarantee you that they'll keep you from buying real estate.

The next time you're in the showroom of your friendly new car dealer, ask yourself, "Am I here buying this car because I need it? Will my family be better off?" Or "Am I buying this car to impress my neighbors and peer group?" When you've answered these questions to your satisfaction, then ask one more question of yourself, "If I give my money to the car dealer, how much investment property is he going to buy with my money?"

This is a *how-to* book. My job is to show you how to make money in the real estate business. I'd also like to show you, in some way, how to manage your money. My advice is this: buying new cars is futile. If you've learned nothing more from this book than this, I've succeeded.

I know I needed a lecture back then, but there was no one around and no how-to book. I was unable to see the truth about this horrendous, meaningless, shallow, status symbol. But I'm here to warn you. Take a hard learned lesson from me. Don't get caught in the car trap; it's the height of stupidity. Remember, we said the real estate business is a brain-power business. Here's a chance to use that intelligence.

One last thing, buy real estate now and someday you can buy, with cash, the finest luxury automobile made. All you need to do is wait. End of car lecture.

WHEN THERE'S A NEED FOR INVESTMENT CAPITAL

I regularly upgrade my apartments. I do so for several reasons:

- The rents can be increased as the property is improved.
- All improvements increase the value of the property for future sales.
- All improvements are part of the tax write-off.

These projects take extra money. For the most part, the income pays the cost of operation; it isn't very often that there's a profit at the end of the year. The profit comes in the form of savings, as I've mentioned before—appreciation, depreciation, and equity. So, where does this extra money come from?

Let me add one point here. If there is a profit after all expenses are paid, I highly recommend putting that profit right back into the business—either in new property or in improving the property you own.

Using Your Own Money for Investments

Should a small independent real estate investor use his own money to renovate and repair real estate and to buy additional properties? This question is especially important if it means taking on more indebtedness. I don't have a clear answer to this question and can only say it's something each individual must consider. I can mention several options.

Let's take a $100,000 investment, financed at 9 percent interest, amortized over 25 years. The payment is $827.98 per month. The total for 25 years is $248,394. Now add only $200 to that payment each month. This amount is about the same amount you invest in an IRA savings. The payment, of course, is then $1,027.98, but the $100,000 mortgage is paid off in 14 years, rather than 25 years. Also, rather than paying $248,394, the total with this additional $200 payment per month is $172,700. In that 14 years you'll have spent $33,600 but have saved $75,693.

Another thought to keep in mind is that if you're a young investor raising a family, it might be best to spend your money on your family. On the other hand, if you are a middle-aged investor buying property during your peak earning years, you might want to get the property paid off more quickly and have the rental income with no mortgage payment.

No matter how you invest the money—the banks, the tenants, or your own—there's no better place in the world to invest than real estate.

It's secure, safe against inflation, has earning power, and has income that can't be taken away.

Taking on More Debt Can be a Tough Decision

Probably as tough a decision as any of us can make is whether we should take on more debt. That's especially true for us who have had to work hard to accumulate and build our security.

As we progress in the real estate business, we'll find times when we need additional money for buying property, renovating property, and buying new appliances and equipment. When this happens, we are besieged with doubt and anxieties. We often think, "Where will the money come from to make the payment?" Or we might think, "What if the tenants quit paying or move out?"

Let me free up your anxieties. If you've invested in the right location, taken care of your property and tenants, have handled your finances in a proper manner, and are not living beyond your means, real estate will take care of itself.

Most of the investors I know have never experienced a rash of vacancies. They've always been able to come up with the money, and they've succeeded.

I have, however, seen some investors who have bought in the wrong community, spent too much on the property, didn't know what they were getting into, were undercapitalized, or lived too extravagantly with the real estate money. They've had vacancies, they've had financial problems, and they've gone broke.

But those of us who've used common sense have avoided most of these problems. The fact is, the good manager using common sense is always on the lookout for good deals. Debt is taken in stride because it means more profits.

My advice then is, when you're making plans for a loan, know what you're doing. Consult with a banker, friend, accountant, associate, or family member. Go over the investment plan and debt repayment plan. Ask advice, especially from those people you respect and trust.

Once you get the feeling that you know what you're doing, that it all looks good, then you're on the way. Go with it. Don't procrastinate. Procrastination only creates more anxieties and an emotional sinkhole. And, *stay away from negative people.*

Seeking Additional Investment Capital

In seeking investment capital, you'll soon discover that money speaks loudly and with power. That power represents the ability to get loans you need. The banker knows this.

Here's why real estate can and will develop borrowing power:

- Equity. Rents, other people's money pays off the mortgage, which builds equity.
- Sweat Equity. Time, work, and effort invested in the property increases its value.
- Appreciation. Time and good care of the property increases its value.
- Inflation. The value of property is increased when inflation increases; no money is involved.

All of these things increase the value of the property. As the value increases so does the borrowing power, which provides the security the banker needs to insure the bank's loan.

Borrowing power certainly provides the capacity to grow in the real estate business. It also puts the investor in a position to make financial dealings that fit investments and debt reduction.

Obviously, we all know that banks are in business to make a profit. That profit is based on points and interest. We've talked about them before. As you can now see, if you have the power, you can demand a loan to fit your needs, including lower interest and no points.

AVOID PARTNERSHIPS

One option some people have used to acquire investment capital is taking on a partner. I'm skeptical and don't recommend this choice, other than in the equity sharing plan. Here's why.

Usually people go into partnerships for financial or managerial support. This support more often than not, does not work out. When the partnership first goes into business, everything is fine. There's a camaraderie and good fellowship. The partners get along well and the work is equally shared. Usually the spouses will pitch in, and everything seems to work well. The partners feel good about each other. This good feeling usually is short-lived, however. One partner eventually sluffs off and doesn't do his share. The other partner takes notice and pretty soon one of the spouses is saying, "Why should we do all the work and not get paid?" Pretty soon there's a breakdown in communications, and the partnership weakens. Subsequently, the purpose of the partnership—moral, financial, managerial, and work support—collapses.

The next stage of events affects the property. It's ignored by all involved. No one takes care of the vacancies. Ultimately the property is vacated and literally becomes worthless. It has to be sold for little or nothing. The result is the real estate is gone, the money is gone, and the friendship is ended.

There's something else to keep in mind regarding a partnership, and that is, you can be held liable for your partners debts. This debt can include personal and business obligations, as well as civil and criminal charges. This fact alone should discourage anyone from thinking about a partnership. Listen, if the deal is good enough for a partnership, it's good enough to go alone.

10

Self-Management
and Sweat Equity
Pay Handsomely

BY NOW YOU SHOULD BE WELL AWARE OF THE FACT THAT YOU'RE ENTER-
ing into, or are in, a dynamic business that can have a dramatic impact
on your future. For this reason, by all means think of real estate as a
business and not a hobby.

When I first went into the business I, more or less, treated it with
a casual attitude. I figured it was something I could do at my leisure—on
weekends, holidays, and vacations. This concept is partially true, because
most of the work can be done on a part-time basis, but it must be treated
with a serious attitude.

Keep your real estate on a business basis, but don't let it interfere
with your personal, home, and family life.

As I accumulated more property, it didn't take long to realize that
property represented quite an investment. The equity began building,
along with the appreciation, and that represented wealth and money.

I quickly discovered that my net worth, at least on paper, was
increasing dramatically. I then decided these investments weren't by any
means a hobby, but a viable and substantial part of my business, savings,
and security.

I'm thankful I took this position, got serious, made some adjustments,
and said to myself, "My gosh, this business is really something else.
I don't know how I could find any better way to save money than buying
and taking care of my real estate." Since then, needless to say, I could
no longer treat this business casually or as a sideline.

The great part of this business is that it can be done on a part-time basis. Here's how it can work. Periodically take a day or weekend to catch up on the various chores. Once they're all caught up, then sit back and relax. Wait until there's another list and do the same thing again. In this way, it doesn't become an overwhelming burden.

Make sure you take care of the various problems because you don't want to let the tenants think you're not concerned about their building. If they get the impression you don't care, they won't care either.

YOUR INVESTMENT IS PRIMARILY TIME AND WORK

As a real estate investor, you're only investment that has created this substantial savings account is your time and work, other than a down payment. Always keep in mind that as long as the rent checks come in each month and pay off your mortgage, then your contribution, that of management, should be easy.

Good management practices can avoid a lot of problems. If you're serious about investing in real estate, then take the time to learn the business and take care of the property. If you don't, it could mean a disastrous financial loss. Here's an example of what I mean.

I know an investor who bought 10 rental units. He did a great job for the first four to five years. Then he got lax and careless about taking care of the property. He let things get run-down, didn't mow the lawns, didn't paint, and neglected the tenant's complaints. Eventually the good tenants moved out and the money quit flowing, and this started an avalanche of trouble. As the problems kept piling up, he lost interest and began treating the property with disdain; in fact, he totally ignored it.

Next, the properties turned into slums. Persistent vacancies existed, and the tenants living there didn't pay their rent because he wouldn't make repairs. The entire operation got out of hand. The last I heard, he was going to let the property go back on foreclosure. It became a virtual sinkhole.

CAN YOU GET RICH QUICK WITH REAL ESTATE?

I wish I could tell you that the real estate business is so good that all you have to do is buy all the property you want, turn it over to a manager, and let the money roll in, and there'd be no problems.

You might think, after watching some of the television real estate promoters, that it doesn't take much to buy, own, manage, and operate property. It's easy to get the impression after watching some of these pitchmen that it's no money down, sign on the dotted line, hire someone to do the work, sit back, collect the rent money, buy a Rolls Royce, and become an overnight millionaire.

Some promoters will tell you that managing your own property is a waste of time. They'll advise you to hire someone to do the work for $10 an hour, and you spend your time buying more real estate and make $500 an hour.

That philosophy of buying real estate might be all right for those who have plenty of cash. Most of us aren't that fortunate, however. A lot of us have had to work for what we've accumulated and found it tough hanging onto that.

I'd like to have found that road to easy wealth, but I didn't. I can further tell you that, from my experience, it's not all that easy to invest and make money in the real estate business. The fact is that self-management is an important part of a successful operation. Let's take a look at what I mean.

DOING IT YOURSELF

I know I told you at the start of this book that 95 percent of your involvement would be mental and about 5 percent physical. With real estate you become involved with both, but you do have a choice and can determine just how much time, work, and effort you want to put into the property. Here's a list of the various duties that can make a difference in the profit:

- Collecting rents
- Bookkeeping
- Paying bills
- Cleaning hallways and laundry room
- Cleaning vacant apartments
- Fixing minor repairs
- Painting
- Mowing lawns
- Shoveling snow

If we don't do the work, what's the alternative? Hired help, which costs part of the profits.

Beware of complacency. In the real estate business, it's pretty easy to become "old, fat, and lazy." Pretty soon we think it's easier to hire someone to do the work. This hired labor takes from the profits!

Real estate managerial firms charge anywhere from 5 to 15 percent of the gross income. Not only is hired management expensive, but hired managers rarely take care of your property as well as you would like. They tend to be more lax, take a shortcut whenever they can, or just don't do whatever needs to be done. Hired managers often overlook repairs until they become real problems. They fix only what has to be fixed and let other things slide.

Repairmen are not cheap. I've been in the real estate business for 25 years and have experienced a moderate amount of success. I could easily afford a repairman. However, as I look at the basic reason for being in the business—profit—I find that being my own manager is the best investment I can make. To this day, I still do some of my own repair work and know this adds to my financial well-being. When I do the repairs, I know they're done right. When the operation is in good order, it's a pleasant experience to be in the real estate business.

There's no doubt in my mind that, if I can do these things, anyone can. Do as I do; learn some repair skills.

Pay yourself for the work you do on your own property and charge it off as an expense. It's tax deductible.

Repair skills can be one of the best money-makers you'll find. A general handyman can do so many things. Let's take a look at some of the simple tasks anyone can do.

Get It Fixed Right the First Time

When fixing and repairing items, make them strong, durable, and long-lasting. Tenants don't take care of things like you do. For instance, if you're putting in a towel rack and it doesn't seem strong, take the time and effort to make it stronger. Maybe it'll mean putting in a larger screw, or whatever. But fix it right the first time or you'll be back later to fix it again. Returning to make repairs is costly, not only financially, but in time and energy. It's what I call "persistant return to a problem burn-out", and it should be avoided.

"Nuts and Bolts" Ideas that Save Time and Money

Don't overfix. You don't need a chandelier when a simple light fixture works. The chandelier won't add to the value of the property, nor will it increase the rents.

When remodeling, buy as many products as possible from sales, such as close out, crazy days, garage, foreclosure, community, church, or any sale for that matter. Always keep your eyes open for building materials. If you don't buy on sale and you use the same hardware, appliance, or lumber dealer all of the time, ask for a discount.

Keep a small tackle box or toolbox filled with assorted screws, bolts, and nuts. They're something you need to keep with you all the time. If you're at an apartment fixing something and don't have your toolbox there, it means a trip to the store.

If you own several apartment units, make a list of the various repairs and tasks. Then pick a day or weekend and do them all at once. Once you get in the swing of things, and start doing the work, everything will begin to flow and work well for you. You'll see progress being made, and you'll feel much better seeing a job done well.

Check each apartment at vacancy time. Keep them fresh, clean, and something you'd live in yourself.

Learn Some Plumbing Skills

Probably 80 percent of all the tenant service calls are for plumbing repairs. Here's what you'll hear:

- The toilet is plugged.
- The sewer is plugged.
- The kitchen or bathroom shower faucet is leaking.
- The hot water is insufficient.

Hired help to fix any of these problems is costly.

I've learned some of the basic plumbing skills so I could take care of these calls. It's not necessary to become a full-fledged plumber, but, there are some things any handyman can do.

The National Retail Hardware Assn., 770 North High School Road, Indianapolis, IN 46224, has 51 "How To" books including *How to Unstop Clogged Drains*, *How to Fix Toilets and Sewers*, etc. These books are comparatively inexpensive. They might also be available at your local library.

Here are some "How To" things anyone can do:

Roto Rooter. Consider buying a small Roto Rooter. Used ones cost about $275. One service call from a professional plumber costs $40 to $80.

Ninety percent of the time the drain is clogged because of tree roots. Simply run the Roto Rooter through once and they're cleaned out. Root killer costs $9.95 per jug. If it's a perpetual problem in one location, have the tenant flush this root killer down the drain every two weeks or so. Be sure it's done at night with the last flush so the killer lays in the drain overnight.

The other 10 percent of the time, it's sanitary napkins that clog the drain. In this case, put a note in each bathroom to the tenants: DO NOT FLUSH SANITARY NAPKINS IN TOILET.

Generic toilet paper doesn't dissolve. Because of this fact, it can get caught in the drainpipe, especially around tree roots. If you have a tenant who uses generic toilet paper, ask him to change to a brand name.

Leaky Faucets. Most leaky faucets are caused by the rubber gasket wearing out. It's a fairly simple job to repair. Keep an assortment of gaskets in your toolbox so you don't have to go to the store every-time you have a leaky faucet to repair. When making this repair be sure to shut off the water before disconnecting the faucet.

Sometimes the entire faucet must be replaced. This replacement takes a little more skill, but can be done.

Toilet Flushers. Again, we are dealing with a rubber product that wears out. It's a fairly simple task to replace a toilet flusher. Be sure to shut off the water, remove the worn-out stopper, and replace it. It costs about $40 to have a plumber do this repair.

Hot-Water Heaters. Hot-water heaters can be repaired. The main cause of a defective water heater is that the electric heating units burn out. They can be replaced by anyone. Here's how. Shut off the water, and turn off the electricity. Take the water pressure off the tank by opening a faucet. It doesn't have to be drained completely. Open the faucet at the bottom of the heater. Take out the electrical unit and re-place it. Sometimes these units are in solid, so it might take a hammer and chisel to get them loose. Be sure to tighten the replacement so you don't have a water leak.

As you can see, repairs can be made without hiring expensive help. There are other simple tasks you can do to save expensive service calls.

KEEPING THE PROPERTY IN GOOD CONDITION

Sometimes we go about our business and don't recognize some of the small repairs we should make. We think nobody notices them. Yet, some of these things, like a dirty toilet seat or a greasy kitchen stove, can turn a prospective tenant immediately. Once they see this dirt and are turned off, they're gone. You don't get a second chance.

It's not only important to keep the premises clean and in good re-pair for prospective tenants, but it has an overall affect on the value of the property. Here's a case in point. I was contacted by a real estate agent on a six-plex that was up for sale. When I first looked at the prop-erty, I thought it was hopeless. Weeds were growing in the yard; the front entry needed painting; the walls in the hallway had chipped paint; the carpet hadn't been cleaned for years; the mail boxes were dented; and the basement was filled with old mattresses, luggage, cans, and other debris tenants had left. It was about at the slum stage.

After looking it over, I came to the conclusion that with some cosmetic work it could be a good investment. Because of it's appearance, the price was fairly low. As a matter of fact, I'm convinced that if the seller had taken the time to fix up a few things, he easily could have sold the prop-erty for several thousand dollars more than he did.

At any rate, I bought the property and since have cleaned, painted, and fixed, and it's turned out to be an excellent investment. The point is, take good care of your property on a regular basis; don't let things accumulate until it's too late.

UPGRADING PROPERTY

Upgrading can be one of the least expensive methods of increasing the property rents and values. Obviously, the better the apartment, the more you can charge for rent.

Most of the projects are comparatively inexpensive and can be done by anyone. Each can have a dramatic affect on the appearance, both inside and out. Let's take a look at some of these things that can change the life of the building:

- A clean yard
- Clean basement
- Clean and well-lit hallways
- Clean carpet
- Washer and dryer service in good repair
- A new toilet seat
- New light fixtures
- A clean refrigerator and stove
- New shades and curtains
- Repair of cracks in walls and ceilings
- New kitchen cupboards to replace old wooden ones

This list of course, doesn't cover all aspects of the upgrading, but you get the general idea.

CUTTING COSTS OF PAINTING

I've purposely left painting to last. Painting certainly is as inexpensive a method of upgrading as you can find.

Not only is it inexpensive but, anyone can paint. Painting can and will add immeasurably to the overall appearance of the property, both inside and outside.

Most people don't like to paint; however, it's something a conservative, or let's say a cheapskate, investor is going to have to do to add to the profit picture. It's a simple fact of life of the real estate investor who wants to make money and get ahead.

You can save time and work when it comes to painting if you follow these simple tips. For instance, by all means get the tenants to do the work whenever you can—and they usually will do it. Offer to buy all the materials if they do the work.

I find that tenants are happy to paint and will do other work if they're asked. I've had tenants shampoo carpet, clean hallways, and do some minor remodeling. I had one tenant who was so good at keeping up his apartment I gave him the okay to put a small workshop in the basement where he kept his tools and equipment. It didn't take long until he was fixing things for other tenants, as well as doing minor repair work around the building. I think he did it because he was treated with the best of consideration, and I certainly let him know I appreciated what he was doing. He never once asked for money.

Now, getting back to painting. If the tenant won't do it, use your family. Avoid hiring professional painters to do the work because it's costly.

Next, go to your paint store and offer to do all your business there. Then ask for a discount. Painting contractors get a discount; ask for the same.

Finally, take good care of your brushes, pans, rollers, and other materials. If you don't, you'll be running to the store for new equipment every time you paint.

Paint with two colors. Use white for the outside of the house, the bathroom, and the kitchen. Everything else should be painted an off-white color. If you paint every building white, you can store what's left over. Also, white doesn't fade like other colors.

I save all the leftovers in a five-gallon plastic pail. If I used different colors on each building, I'd have a lot of leftover pails of colored paint. This procedure applies to the interior paint, as well as the exterior paint.

Leftovers can be used for the interior to fill in the nail holes and spot paint when a tenant moves out. It's also easy to paint over the soiled areas. If you use only one color, when an apartment has to be repainted, it only requires one coat.

I'm convinced that one of the best clues to a good buy is a bad paint job. Therefore, if you intend to sell, be sure the building is freshly painted.

REPLACING CARPETING

An inexpensive replacement is carpeting. When it's worn out and dirty, replace it. Tenants look at the carpeting right away. New carpeting can make the inside of an apartment look fresh and new.

Always look for bargains—not only of carpeting, but all materials.

GETTING BIDS

When upgrading property, whether it's a major overhaul, revamping of the interior, installation of new electrical service, or general work, get more than one bid. If you don't get more than one bid, it's possible that your one and only friendly contractor will eventually take advantage of this friendship and start charging a little more than he should. Bids will keep that contractor honest, whether he's a friend or not.

———————

Clearly, one of the best money-makers in the real estate business is in renovating older properties. Look into this possibility as an investment program, if you've the time and energy.

———————

11

Managing
Real Estate
through a Crisis

IT WOULD BE NICE TO HAVE A 100 PERCENT GUARANTEE THAT EVERY property we bought was a good buy, that there'd be no problems, that every investment would be a money-maker, and that there'd be no financial setbacks. I wish I could report that every real estate deal is a bed of roses.

It also would be nice if we could inherit enough money so we could invest in mortgage-free real estate with no debt, and plenty of rent to cover any financial problems. But as you and I know, very few of us get this kind of start. Realistically, we know this isn't the way things happen, and it's not the real world of real estate.

The fact is, in the real world of real estate, there are some bad buys, poor investments, and financial problems that can cause trouble. Following is a list of things that can contribute to a negative investment:

- High purchase price
- Defective property
- Insufficient income to cover expenses
- Value decreases dramatically after purchase
- Costly repairs not anticipated
- Unforseen high vacancies
- Overrenovating older property causing increased debt load
- Consistant chronic repairs
- A need for refinancing

- Interest too high
- Payment too high
- Job change
- Leaving community and hiring expensive management
- Insurance loss with inadequate coverage

There's also the ever-present threat of taking rent money and:

- Buying a Mazeratti instead of a Ford
- Spending reserve cash held for taxes and spending it on personal expenditures
- Living a lifestyle off the real estate income

CHOOSE A COMMON-SENSE ROAD TO RECOVERY

When most of us invest in real estate, we experience great exhilaration once the rent money starts rolling in. It's like that Great American Dream come true. There's all that money and it seems so spendable. Some of us will let our spending of this money get out of hand. We spend it on other things, rather than paying the real estate bills. Pretty soon we're in financial trouble and eventually a sinkhole.

Don't let this happen. Be certain the rent money is put away for paying the bills—first. Remember that most rental property doesn't make any profit for the first three or four years, so every penny of income is needed just to break even.

Take my advice and set up a real estate budget. Make a financial analysis of the operation. Know what money you need and when you need it. Don't overlook any of the following expenses when establishing a budget:

- Interest and principal on loan payment
- Insurance
- Taxes
- Utilities
- Cleaning and maintenance
- Legal and bookkeeping
- Repairs
- Supplies
- Labor
- Fuel
- Soft water
- Garbage
- Advertising and promotion

- Dues and memberships
- Refunds

Solving a Cash-flow Problem

If there's insufficient income to cover the expenses, find out the cause and get it corrected immediately. For instance, if the cost of heat or utilities is higher than you had expected, find a way to cut the costs. If you pay the heat in an apartment building, you'll find the tenants will open a window in the middle of winter to cool down the apartment. If this is the case, ask for the tenants' cooperation.

To save on a utility bill, you might need to put in smaller light bulbs in the halls and basement. Possibly you'll have to increase the washer/dryer service from $.50 to $.75 or whatever. These changes might seem stingy, but it's a case of saving pennies and the dollars will count up.

Following are some other tasks that you can do to help the cash flow.

Cut Costs By Doing Your Own Work. Rather than calling an expensive service or repair person, go to your apartment and see if you can make the necessary repairs. You'd be surprised how many things can be repaired without calling expensive service people.

Increase Income By Raising Rent to Save the Investment. If rent isn't high enough to cover expenses, raise it. Don't price yourself out of the market, though.

It's difficult to continue raising rents. Eventually, the tenants will look elsewhere. At a time when the income is needed because of other financial difficulties, the last thing you need is vacancies.

How to determine and charge the *right* amount of rent is a crucial part of real estate management—something you'll learn. A part of that management skill is to learn not to charge too much and create vacancies. On the other hand, you must learn how to charge enough, in order to have sufficient income to pay the expenses.

When you are deciding what rent to charge, you must find out what the traffic will bear. This skill is a primary concern of management. What do other apartment owners charge? The best way to learn this fact is to talk to other investors in your community. Here's an example of what I mean.

I own a property in a large city. Whenever I have a vacancy, I call a friend who owns a number of apartment complexes. These people, active in the business every day, know the market. I tell them what kind of unit I have and ask what they think is a fair rent for it. They do not think of me as a competitor, so they give advice freely. Their answers are honest and helpful 99 percent of the time. If I'm not quite sure of their response, I'll call another investor. Eventually, after several calls, I'll get a pretty good estimate and go with that.

Incidentally, this is an example of how much good can develop from becoming an active member of an apartment association in your city, neighborhood, or community.

In addition to this source of help and information, there's another way to determine rents and that is to check the newspaper for rent ads. Find an advertisement that appears to be comparable to your apartment; then call as though you're a prospective tenant and ask how much the apartment rent is. With a little assertive investigative work, you should come up with an answer.

Extend Payment—Seek a New Loan. If there's a short-term mortgage with a quick payoff, the payments might be too high. In this case, contact the banker or contract holder and ask for extended payments or a new loan with new terms and smaller payments. Sometimes, just alleviating one or two month's payments can put you back on track.

The possibility also exists, if there's sufficient equity, of getting a second mortgage on the property. A second mortgage should be undertaken with a full understanding that the payments can be met on time, and that it's an emergency situation.

Another Alternative: Get Out Quickly

If the deal is bad, if it's not going to work, if there's insufficient income to cover the expenses, and if there's no way of getting refinancing, consider turning the property back either on a voluntary basis through an agreement with the mortgage holder, or through foreclosure.

Keep in mind that if you turn the property back, you can be held liable for some of the losses. If you have a contract for deed with a $50,000 balance, and if you turn the property back to the contract holder, and if he can only sell the property for $40,000, he can come back and hold you responsible for the $10,000. If this situation should occur, be sure you have good legal representation and advice.

In fact, before getting into any foreclosure, you'll want to have an attorney to help you make the decision. Foreclosure is an alternative only if it looks like a totally disasterous situation that can't be corrected any other way.

DON'T TAKE THE OBLIGATION OF DEBT LIGHTLY

Debt should not be taken lightly. It must be paid back. Many investors have gone broke because they couldn't and didn't control debt. Going through financial growing pains can be difficult for any small business, whether it's for improving property, or buying additional property.

There's only one person in a small real estate business operation who can solve any of the financial problems, take the blame, correct the errors, and make sure the operation is running smoothly. I'm sure you know who I mean.

BANKRUPTCY IS NOT AN ALTERNATIVE

Bankruptcy has become very easy and almost acceptable. It's the thing to do, like a status symbol. You almost see people *honored* after filing bankruptcy.

Many people out there will tell you to get rid of your financial problems by filing for bankruptcy. They'll tell you it's easy and inexpensive, and you can file bankruptcy and start all over again. Some will even tell you that it will not affect your credit record. Others will charge you a fee and promise to get it off your credit record. *Wrong!*

Bankruptcy will remain a permanent part of your credit file for *ten* years. Not only will it have an affect on all your future credit buying, but it will definitely affect your real estate investing.

For instance, a bankruptcy on your record will keep you from obtaining an FHA or VA mortgage, as well as a Visa, Master Card, or American Express credit card. Most major mail-order and department stores will refuse to issue a credit card to anyone with a bankruptcy. It's not worth the problems you will encounter.

In all the years I've been involved in business, I've never seen one legitimate bankruptcy. Do you know why? Because 99 percent of the bankruptcies can be attributed to one of the following:

- Greed
- Squandering
- Poor management
- Overspending
- Gross financial irresponsibility

The 1 percent of legitimate bankruptcies is for catastrophic illness and extreme medical costs.

When you come right down to it, a bankruptcy is no more than a legal document to steal—steal someone's hard-earned money. Usually, it involves money from innocent victims. Some of these victims have worked hard to acquire their money. Once the bankruptcy is filed, there's no way they can recover their money. It's gone.

Good investors, good managers, and *good people* don't let themselves get into a position in which they have to file bankruptcy. Be a good investor, not a bankrupt one.

COMPETENT FINANCIAL CONTROL CAN AVOID A DISASTER

Let's go back to our friend Benjamin Franklin, who said, "Watch the pennies, and the dollars take care of themselves." This advice is the best advice anyone can give.

Actually, it's difficult to find strong enough words to make a strong enough impression of the importance of financial responsibility.

Financial responsibility is extremely important because it literally is the *key* to the success or failure of the real estate business, or any other business for that matter. The bankruptcy courts are filled with small business managers who have gone broke because of a lack of financial accountability and responsibility.

For some reason, when some of us experience even a modicum of success, there seems to be an immediate departure from common-sense fiscal management. Quick and easy money is a new experience. Quite frankly, it's an experience that a lot of us can't comprehend. It can be awesome.

THE FINANCIAL SINKHOLE THAT CAN LEAD TO FAILURE

That awesomeness comes from the fact that the extra money coming in at the beginning of each month looks like it's all free and clear. Sometimes we ignore, consciously or unconsciously, the cost of operation. We think, "I'll just spend a little and nobody will notice." Sometimes we'll spend the money and say to ourselves, "I'll make up the money for the real estate tax later."

Next we discover we're in debt, and now it's time to get back on the road to recovery. So we make a quick trip to the bank. We say to ourselves, rather deceitfully, "That's easy. We'll make the payment later with the rent money." That's the beginning of a financial sinkhole and eventually, if it's not taken under control, it becomes a disaster.

What occurs next is the one thing that causes more business failures than anything else in the business world: *personal overspending.*

This fact is so important that it bears repeating: *the number one cause of business failure is personal overspending.*

Personal overspending is the most pathetic sinkhole you can get into. Avoid it like the plague. If you're faced with financial difficulties, don't let false pride get in your way. Communicate with someone about your problems.

Those with whom you'll discuss these problems will most likely be the most compassionate, the most understanding, and the most helpful. Not only can they help you with much-needed advice, but they can be emotionally supportive when it's most needed. Just someone to talk with can alleviate a lot of the pressures and anxieties.

If you see a crisis coming or if you're in the middle of a crisis, don't ignore it; don't let it linger and fester. Make your decision of what has to be done to solve it, and then do it! Ignoring it only creates anxieties and headaches.

Whatever you do, don't let problems remain unsolved and end up with sleepless nights and ultimately in the grave.

I've mentioned before in this book—seek help. Use a friend, fellow investor, family member, or banker. The banker usually won't charge for his advice. If you need professional help, that of an accountant or attorney, expect to pay, but regardless, seek help.

How to Take Control of Your Personal Finances

I suppose if I had a pat answer on how to control personal overspending that worked, I'd be a millionaire many times over by selling this information.

The truth is, I don't have a pat answer, nor does anyone else. That answer can only come from the individual involved—the overspender. In most cases, the answer comes when it hurts enough and something has to be done—if it's not too late.

The easiest way to solve the problem of a financial sinkhole, of course, is not to get into one in the first place. But that's easier said than done. I suppose, for those of us who have struggled on the way up to get where we want to be (financially speaking) and we see all those trappings—cars, status symbols, and what have you—we want them, and want them now. The unfortunate part of that sinkhole, however, is that we want them before our time and we want them whether we can afford them or not. Caution and concern are thrown to the wind.

My advice then is to be careful; spend and live within your means. Don't try to keep up with the country club set, until you're ready. Then you can buy the country club.

To get the business in line, set up a budget and live by it. In the real estate business you know you have bills to pay, including insurance and taxes. If the insurance and taxes cost $2,400 a year, put aside $200 a month. Put it in a savings account where it'll earn interest. In a savings account it might not be quite as easy to get at as in a checking account. *Don't* spend this money for other things and think you'll make it up later.

Operating a business shrewdly is almost instinctive, or, as my friend says, "You're a cheapskate." Yes, maybe I am, but I do know those conservative, nonspending methods work and help build a secure future.

Incidentally, my friends don't see me when I'm going first class and enjoying the warm beaches of some exotic island. They can't afford to get there—even coach class.

I'll guarantee you that, if you're patient, take your time, live within your means, spend wisely, and invest shrewdly, in good time you'll be able to go first class.

BEWARE OF THE "CADILLAC" IMAGE

There's no sense asking for trouble you don't need. I figure if you're driving a Cadillac and should be in a Ford or Chevrolet, you're asking for trouble. When you do drive that Cadillac and you should be in the Ford, most people know this, so you're not fooling anyone but yourself. You're not going to impress anyone, and it seems to me that it's just too costly a status symbol. Quite frankly, if you're a beginner in the real estate business, you don't need these things.

These status symbols only cause trouble. I know of one individual who had operated a small business, including some investment property. However, his life-style grew faster than his money, which means he spent more than he was making. Ultimately, the business failed because of his high living and personal overspending. The irony of this whole story is that, after all that despair—going broke, losing all the real estate and his business—Mr. Status Seeker drove from his foreclosed home to his rented apartment in a Cadillac. He just couldn't give up that false hopeless image.

So take heed. Don't overspend or overextend your life-style and live beyond your means. If you're in financial trouble, get control of it. Get rid of the Cadillacs in your life and get your priorities straight. Think financial security first, then think Cadillac.

HINDSIGHT CONTROL OF FINANCES DOESN'T WORK

It's easy to see anyone's past failures—better known as *hindsight management*. We're all experts at it. It doesn't take any intellectual whiz to look back at someone with that Cadillac image and say, "He shouldn't have done it."

The answers and solutions to financial problems must come from more than hindsight, however. They are a combination of understanding the cause of these failures, learning from those who've experienced failure, and then creating within ourselves some foresight, rather than hindsight. It's better to know the answers before the problems arise. Therein lies the key to good managerial skills. It's knowing how to manage and eliminate any possibility of a crisis.

TIME IS ON YOUR SIDE

With real estate, any sort of setback is temporary. Prices of investment property, as well as rents, are constantly in a state of flux. Most of the time that movement is on an uphill swing, which means real estate all by itself, along with good management, will create more value, more income, and less chance of failure.

If you experience a temporary setback, time will be on your side. If you can get through it, the real estate will take care of itself.

Patience is a virtue you'll want to nurture with real estate.

12

Tenants:
The Lifeblood
of the
Real Estate Business

CERTAINLY THE MAJORITY OF REAL ESTATE INVESTORS WILL TELL YOU that good tenants are the most important ingredient of a profitable, smooth-operating real estate business.

Whether you select your tenants or hire someone to do it for you, make certain it's done right so you get the best.

Tenants can literally make or break an investment business. This fact not only applies to how they pay their rent, but how they take care of the property. They are, in fact, the *life blood of the real estate investment business.*

Think of it this way. Tenants pay for *your* investment. Their rent pays all the bills, which includes interest, taxes, utilities, upkeep, maintenance, and the payment on *your* mortgage. That mortgage payment builds equity, and equity is security.

It's not hard to conclude that the better the tenant, the more profitable the venture and the better the operation. With a good operation, you eliminate headaches. As I've said before, eliminating headaches is one of the goals of this book.

I wish I could tell you that you can just rent at random to anyone who comes along, and there'd be no problems or nuisances. That's not the real world of real estate, however. Problems and nuisances do exist. You can avoid them, though, if you screen and select tenants with the ultimate care.

SCREENING TENANTS

Screening tenants isn't that difficult, but it takes some assertive measures to get the job done correctly. Assertiveness is a necessary part of this business.

Develop a reputation of being a *first-class* landlord. The word gets around and when it does, you'll get the calls from the first-class tenants.

Some of the nice-guy managers I've known take the first tenant who calls. They want to keep the image of being a nice guy and not turn anyone down. Their first mistake is not taking time to screen and check the credit and references of the potential tenant. So what happens? Unreliable tenants get into the apartment, don't pay the rent, and are slovenly in housekeeping. The next thing you know, Joe Nice Guy is out there cleaning up and repairing a vacant apartment and trying to collect past-due rent. Sometimes he ends up digging into the profits of the business, or his own pockets for that matter, to cover the expenses—all because he didn't select with care. The nice-guy image remains, but the tenant got away with his money. That just doesn't make common sense.

ADS FOR VACANCIES

My theory about running newspaper advertisements for vacancies is to make the ad as simple as possible. For instance, simply use this: ''One- (or two, whatever) bedroom apartment for rent. Call (your telephone number)''

If you put too much information in the ad, some good potential tenant might not call. By leaving out the information, more people will call and, in this way, you can screen them accordingly.

The way to word your advertisements is something you as an investor can experiment with. It's something you might want to talk about with other investors. Also, your own community, city, or neighborhood can make a difference.

COMMON SENSE CAN HELP AVOID PROBLEMS

Rule Number One: Check and Screen the Tenants. Know who you're renting to. Eliminate the problem tenants before they get settled in. I'll show you how later.

Rule Number Two: Take Your Time. Most of us have a tendency to rent to the first caller in response to our ad—like Joe Nice Guy. We don't seem to have the ability to say ''no'' when the first call comes in. I suppose we're afraid we won't get the apartment rented, so we make a commitment before making a sound, common-sense, rational judgement. I repeat, *take your time*. Remember, that ad can run longer in the paper and there will be other calls.

One of the greatest invisible assets of real estate investing is *time*. No matter what happens with your investment, *time* is on your side.

Rule Number Three: Proceed with a Thorough Investigation of the Potential Tenant. Conducting the investigation, which I'll show you how to do, is not so time-consuming, is comparatively inexpensive, and really pays in the long run.

Rule Number Four: Conduct a Thorough Telephone Interview. Start the telephone interview by being assertive. Be in charge of the call and the caller right from the start. Don't let the caller get ahead of you with his questions.

Handle it this way: The person will invariably ask, "Can you tell me about the apartment?" or "How much is the rent?" or any number of questions.

Before giving him an answer, give him your name and no other information. Then ask, "Who's this speaking?" Expect and wait for an answer. If he doesn't want to give you his name, forget about him and wait for the next call. Again, know to whom you're renting.

If the caller gives you his name, write it down and proceed with the next questions, which should be: "How many people is this for?" In this way, you'll find out if it's a single person or a family.

Next ask, "Who do you work for?" Be insistent on getting an answer. This information is something you'll definitely want to know. Sometimes you'll get a response like, "What difference does it make where I work?" Tell him, "I'm sure you understand that I want to know who I'm renting to."

Sometimes a caller will just hang up, for any number of reasons. Usually it's because he doesn't want to give you some negative information and, in the long run, you're probably better off.

At this time in the interview, you might want to make the following statement: "I don't allow any loud parties, loud stereo, or mismanaged pets." Add to that, "If you think this doesn't fit your life-style, then maybe it's best that you look elsewhere."

Ninety-nine percent of the time, this works out for both you and the potential tenant. If it's a good tenant, he'll usually say, "I'm looking for a quiet place to live and don't want to be where there are loud parties."

Along the way you'll want to find out if the caller is interested in a long-term or short-term lease.

You should obtain sufficient information to know whether you want to pursue the interview. The information you should gather so far tells where the tenant works, the size of the family, and how long they intend to stay.

Everytime someone moves out of an apartment, it costs money to prepare it for the next tenant. Therefore, long-term leases make sense and are money-makers.

PURSUE THE GOOD TENANT WITH VIGOR

If the preliminary information produces a good potential tenant, give him your best sales pitch, along with complete details about the apartment.

Next, set up an interview at the apartment. Before going on the interview, call the Credit Bureau and find out if that person will pay the rent. If he checks out as a good risk, you're on the way.

When you set up the appointment to see the apartment, do it on your terms. If you don't, you can spend a lot of time waiting. Some people will tell you they'll meet you at 4:00 and not show up until 5:00. Some won't show up at all.

Many real estate managers will say, "I'll meet you at the apartment," then they will sit and wait. Make arrangements to meet that person at your place of business, your home, or wherever it's convenient for you; then go to the apartment together.

In the meantime, if you need more time to investigate or you're not ready to make a commitment, tell the person you'll get back to him. If he doesn't check out and you don't want him, just don't call back.

Never close a rental agreement or take an advertisement out of the paper until you've received the rent deposit or a signed lease.

Some other necessary stall techniques can be used, like: "The apartment isn't ready to show yet," "Someone else on the list ahead of you is still interested." or, you can ask the tenant for references and tell him you'll get back to him as soon as they're checked out.

Remember, you have a right to rent your apartment to anyone you wish. The potential tenant can turn down your apartment; conversely you can turn him down, with the exception of discriminating on the basis of color, race, religion, sex, or creed.

Keep in mind that tenants have legal rights too.

You might not want to rent to some tenants for various reasons. They can be screened at the time of the interview.

Here's what I mean. I have a friend who won't rent to transients—job movers and seasonal workers. He seems to think they will be in the area only for a short time, some of them leaving without giving notice, and some not paying their rent. Those are headaches and problems anyone can do without.

The large corporate real estate firms go through a thorough investigation and screening process before they sign a lease. They don't take chances; nor should you.

GOVERNMENT-SUBSIDIZED HOUSING

The government has subsidized apartment owners to take care of the poor and underprivileged (Fig. 12-1). You, as a taxpayer, help pay for these apartments. Because they are government subsidized, let it be known that it's *their obligation* to provide housing for the needy. They

Fig. 12-1. Housing units, both private and government owned, are located in every community throughout the country. They are built for economically needy families.

should be held responsible to do so. Refer anyone needing financial assistance to these apartment owners.

PET OWNERS

The tenant who owns pets can be troublesome. Pets can be a problem no matter what that person will tell you. They'll say things like, "Oh, my pet's well trained." "You don't have to worry about my dog," or any number of other things. The pets usually aren't as good as they say cats urinate and dogs leave a big mess in the yard and also bark and bite. If you have no-pet policy, stick with it.

On the other hand, if you own a number of apartment buildings, you might consider having one building for pet owners. I'm sure you can charge more rent to the pet owners.

BENEFITS AND LIABILITIES OF STUDENT TENANTS

I have a number of friends who own real estate in college towns. Here's what one said, "Those college parties are wild and go on all hours of the night. There's loud stereo, screaming girls, and plenty of beer to keep up the high pitch." He goes on to say, "It's not a matter of whether there's going to be a party; it's just a matter of when." He told me that party-going and hell-raising tenants can create a lot of headaches in the real estate apartment business.

I have a friend who owns a four-plex near a college campus. She told me she's done pretty well over the years and in general has rented to upperclassmen and graduate students. However, one year she said, "What the heck, I've done well by college students, I'll rent to new students as they come in."

Later she said, "That turned out to be my first mistake. They turned out to be real hell-raisers. Seems like some of them have just left their mother's skirts, probably nagged and suppressed for 17 or 18 years and now by god they're gonna take it out on someone or something." What she found out was that they took it out on her apartments. This abuse included things like fists through the walls, sinks pulled off, broken windows, and a general unkept apartment.

Here's another horror story that happened to a friend of mine. He rented a three-bedroom apartment to college students. About the middle of the cold winter quarter, they decided it was time to have a beach party. Well, you know what a beach party means—it means sand and water. They laid down a plastic covering over the living room floor, hauled in loads of sand, then filled the area with water. You can image how that ended up—very costly to the owner, who is still trying to collect for damages.

One more experience follows, so you have a pretty good idea of what to expect. This owner rented out two units to students. Before the first quarter was over, the students decided that it would be easier to communicate if they knocked out a wall between the two apartments. They did, and my friend didn't discover it until the year was over.

Summer-school students usually are temporary, while the dorms are closed. They move in in June and out in September. These are short terms and it's costly to have tenants move in and out.

On the other hand, there are some excellent student tenants. It's like any other category, however; you must check them out. Avoid the problems before they occur.

TENANTS WORTHY OF CONSIDERATION

You're probably saying by now, "There's nobody left!" I can assure you that there are a lot of outstanding tenants out there—and you want them. As a matter of fact, only bout 20 percent of the tenants cause all the problems. You want to look for, and rent to, the other 80 percent. Let's see who they are.

Like any other business, there's competition in the apartment business. Consider this when you market yourself and your apartment.

Retired Persons, Single and Married. These people make outstanding tenants. If you can provide them with good housing, you can expect them to stay for years. They take excellent care of *their* home— often better than the owner. They are not demanding and are always right on time with the rent. There's no doubt in my mind: they are some of the best and certainly receive a four-star rating in my book of recommendations.

Young Professionals and Semiprofessional Male and Female Workers. This category includes teachers, nurses, college faculty, dental assistants, secretaries, bank clerks, office workers, assistant managers, etc. Most are sophisticated and reliable, take good care of their apartment, pay their rent on time, and in general, are fair and understanding. I highly recommend this group.

Remember, your apartment is *their* home. It's a possession in which they want to take pride.

Young Married Couples. Young marrieds have the same qualities and traits as the young professionals, and in fact most are young professionals. However, they eventually will be looking for larger apartments or buying homes, so they can be temporary tenants. Also, eventually young married couples will have children, and there can be some conflict between young children and retired people.

Serious Students. Juniors, seniors, and post-graduate students all make good tenants, take their school seriously, and in general, are more mature.

Others also qualify as good tenants, but, this list gives you a good idea of what to look for.

One last note: If you get a good tenant, take good care of him. Keep him happy and satisfied. It's to your financial benefit, as well as your peace of mind. Peace of mind, along with good tenants, can eliminate a lot of the headaches of the real estate business.

Treat your tenants with the highest respect and consideration.

RENT DEPOSITS: A MUST PROTECTION

Rent deposits are a must. They are like insurance. These deposits can protect you against property damage, breakage, cleanup, garbage removal, and past-due rents. Tenants leave all sorts of things when they move. If they're not held responsible for the cleanup, it can be an added expense you don't need. Once a tenant has cleaned the apartment, be sure to conduct an onsight inspection before refunding the rent deposit.

Deposit the money in a money market account, which earns interest and is readily available. Remember, rent deposits must be returned to tenants when they move out—minus any costs for breakage, cleanup, etc.

LEASES

A lease is basically a contract between the landlord and the tenant. In general, anything can be put in a lease, all the way from the amount of the rent to who's responsible for garbage.

Often, leases aren't all that effective. If a person's going to move out, he's going to move out. But leases can offer a lot of protection.

Probably an entire book could be printed showing the different type leases. At any rate, Fig. 12-2 and Fig. 12-3 are examples of standard landlord and tenant leases.

THIS INDENTURE, Made this .... day of .... 19........
by and between ....
.... party of the first part, Lessor...... and
of .... party of the second part, Lessee.....
WITNESSETH, That said party of the first part, in consideration of the rents and covenants, hereinafter mentioned, to be paid and performed by said party of the second part, does hereby Demise, Lease and Let unto the said party of the second part, and the said party of the second part does hereby hire and take from the said party of the first part the following described premises, situate in the ....
County of .... and State of .... to-wit:
Apartment numbered .... on .... floor of the
.... situate

to be occupied as and for a dwelling and for no other purpose.
TO HAVE AND TO HOLD, The above rented Apartment to the said party of the second part, his heirs and assigns, for and during the full term of .... year...... from and after the first
day of ....19........ to and until the last day of .... 19........

And the said party of the second part, for himself, his heirs and assigns, agrees to and with the said party of the first part, to pay him, his heirs or assigns, as rent for the above mentioned Apartment, the sum of ....
.... DOLLARS,
in equal monthly payments of .... Dollars per month, from
....

payable in advance at the office of ....
.... on the first day of each and

every month for and during the full term of this Lease.
SAID PARTY OF THE SECOND PART ALSO COVENANTS AND AGREES AS FOLLOWS: To comply with any printed or typewritten regulations now made and posted in the rear halls or basement of said premises, or hereafter to be made and so posted, relating to the use of said building.

To keep premises in as good condition as they now are, or may be put into by said party of the first part, ordinary wear resulting from careful usage and damage by the elements without fault on part of party of the second part, alone excepted.

To drive no nails or screws, or their equivalent, into the walls, ceiling, woodwork, or floors of said premises, or make any change in the internal structure of said building, or any room therein.

To not sell or assign this lease or sublet the said premises, or any part thereof, to any person without first obtaining the written consent of said party of the first part.

To use gas stoves only for cooking; all gas for fuel or light to be paid for by party of the second part.

To permit no noise or nuisance whatever on said premises to the disturbance of other tenants, or keep any animals on said premises.

To comply in all respects with any policy of insurance now upon or covering said premises, or which may hereafter be put upon the same, nor permit anything to be done at or within said leased premises which shall vitiate or increase the current rate of insurance thereon, or upon property kept therein.

To take good care of and keep said premises so as not to endanger the same, or any co-tenants thereon.

To make no claim, and lessee hereby expressly waives any and all claims against said lessor for or on account of any personal injury sustained, or any loss or damage to property, caused by fire, water, deluge or overflow, or explosion, howsoever arising or caused or being within said premises; or for loss of any articles by theft or from any cause, from said premises or building.

No repairs or alterations shall be made except with the full knowledge and consent of said party of the first part. Lessee to be responsible for and mend at his own proper cost, any and all breakage or damage done to any part of premises hereinbefore mentioned, of whatever nature. To replace with as good quality and size, and make good at his own expense, any glass broken on said premises during the continuance of this lease (said glass now being whole).

To care for waxed floors in said apartments properly, allowing no water to be used thereon.

To allow no baby carriages or go-carts or other obstructions to be left standing in the public halls or vestibules in said building.

That said Lessee will not allow any liquors or beverages of an intoxicating nature or tendency to be sold on said premises, nor any gambling nor other immoral practice.

To permit party of the first part, by his officers or agents, to enter said premises at all reasonable times, to view them or to show them to parties wishing to lease or make improvements thereon; and at the expiration of the time herein recited quietly yield and surrender said premises to said party of the first part, his heirs or assigns, in such condition as herein covenanted.

PROVIDED, That if said premises shall be destroyed by fire, this lease shall terminate, but without rebate of rent paid, or due and unpaid; that should party of the second part, his heirs, executors, administrators or assigns, fail to make the above mentioned payments as herein specified, or to pay any of the rent aforesaid when due, or shall fail to fulfill any of the covenants or agreements herein contained, then and in that case it shall be lawful for the said party of the first part, his heirs or assigns, to declare this lease at an end, and re-enter and take possession of said premises, and to hold and retain the same fully and absolutely without such re-entry working a forfeiture of the rents to be paid and the covenants to be performed by the said party of the second part during the full term of this lease.

It is expressly agreed that there shall be no surrender of said premises before the expiration of this lease by party of the second part, except by written consent thereto, hereon, signed by party of the first part. Second party further agrees to give party of the first part written notice thirty days before the expiration of this lease of his intention to vacate at the end of this lease, otherwise party of the first part will have option of continuing this lease for one year from such expiration without notice to party of the second part.

Gas range furnished by first party to be kept in order by second party.

Party of first part agrees to furnish heat for heating said premises from ....

Party of the first part also to furnish lighting fixtures, window shades and screens for all rooms, and gas and gas globes and shades now being whole, and to be replaced if broken by second party.

Hot and cold water to be furnished by party of the first part, but in case of waste or unnecessary use it shall be paid for thereafter by second party at regular rate charged by water company.

Fig. 12-2. An apartment lease.

In Testimony Whereof, *Both parties have hereunto set their hands and seals the day and year hereinbefore written.*

In Presence of

....

....

....

....

....

APARTMENT LEASE

FROM

Lessor

To

Lessee

Amount. $.............*per month*

payable.................

at.................

RESIDENTIAL LEASE-RENTAL AGREEMENT AND DEPOSIT RECEIPT

RECEIVED FROM _____ hereinafter referred to as Tenant,

the sum of $ _____ (_____ DOLLARS),

evidenced by _____ , as a deposit which, upon acceptance of this rental agreement, the Owner

of the premises, hereinafter referred to as Owner, shall apply said deposit as follows:

	DEPOSIT RECEIVED	BALANCE OWING PRIOR TO OCCUPANCY
Rent for the period from _____ to _____	$ _____	$ _____
Security deposit (not applicable toward last month's rent) _____	$ _____	$ _____
Other _____	$ _____	$ _____
TOTAL _____	$ _____	$ _____

In the event that this agreement is not accepted by the Owner or his authorized agent, within _____ days, the total deposit received shall be refunded.

Tenant hereby offers to rent from the Owner the premises situated in the City of _____ , County of _____ ,

State of _____ , described as _____ , consisting of _____

upon the following TERMS and CONDITIONS:

TERM: The term hereof shall commence on _____ , 19 _____ , and continue (check one of the two following alternatives):

☐ until _____ 19 _____ , for a total rent of $ _____ . (_____ dollars).

☐ on a month-to-month basis thereafter, until either party shall terminate the same by giving the other party _____ days written notice delivered by certified mail.

RENT: Rent shall be $ _____ per month, payable in advance, upon the _____ day of each calendar month to Owner or

his authorized agent, at the following address: _____

or at such other places as may be designated by Owner from time to time. In the event rent is not paid within five (5) days after due date. Tenant agrees to pay a late charge

of $ _____ plus interest at _____% per annum on the delinquent amount. Tenant agrees further to pay $_____ for each dishonored bank check.
The late charge period is not a grace period, and Owner is entitled to make written demand for any rent unpaid on the second day of the rental period. Any unpaid balances
remaining after termination of occupancy are subject to 1½% interest per month or the maximum rate allowed by law.

MULTIPLE OCCUPANCY: It is expressly understood that this agreement is between the Owner and each signatory individually and severally. In the event of default by any
one signatory each and every remaining signatory shall be responsible for timely payment of rent and all other provisions of this agreement.

UTILITIES: Tenant shall be responsible for the payment of all utilities and services, except _____

shall be paid by Owner.

USE: The premises shall be used exclusively as a residence for no more than _____ persons. Guests staying more than a total of _____ days in a
calendar year will be considered occupants.

PETS: No pets shall be brought on the premises without the prior written consent of the Owner.

HOUSE RULES: In the event that the premises are a portion of a building containing more than one unit, Tenant agrees to abide by any and all house rules, whether promul-
gated before or after the execution hereof, including, but not limited to, rules with respect to noise, odors, disposal of refuse, pets, parking, and use of common areas Tenant
shall not have a waterbed on the premises without prior written consent of the Owner.

ORDINANCES AND STATUTES: Tenant shall comply with all statutes, ordinances and requirements of all municipal, state and federal authorities now in force or which
may hereafter be in force, pertaining to the use of the premises.

ASSIGNMENT AND SUBLETTING: Tenant shall not assign this agreement or sublet any portion of the premises without prior written consent of the Owner.

MAINTENANCE, REPAIRS OR ALTERATIONS: Tenant acknowledges that the premises are in good order and repair, unless otherwise indicated herein. Owner may at
any time give Tenant a written inventory of furniture and furnishings on the premises and Tenant shall be deemed to have possession of all said furniture and furnishings in
good condition and repair, unless he objects thereto in writing within five (5) days after receipt of such inventory. Tenant shall, at his own expense, and at all times, maintain
the premises in a clean and sanitary manner including all equipment, appliances, furniture and furnishings therein and shall surrender the same, at termination hereof, in
as good condition as received, normal wear and tear excepted. Tenant shall be responsible for damages caused by his negligence and that of his family or invitees and
guests. Tenant shall not paint, paper or otherwise redecorate or make alterations to the premises without the prior written consent of the Owner. Tenant shall irrigate and
maintain any surrounding grounds, including lawns and shrubbery, and keep the same clear of rubbish or weeds if such grounds are a part of the premises and are
exclusively for the use of the Tenant. Tenant shall not commit any waste upon said premises, or any nuisance or act which may disturb the quiet enjoyment of any tenant in
the building.

INVENTORY: Any furnishings and equipment to be furnished by Owner shall be set out in a special inventory. The inventory shall be signed by both Tenant and Owner
concurrently with this Lease and shall be a part of this Lease.

DAMAGES TO PREMISES: If the premises are so damaged by fire or from any other cause as to render them untenantable, then either party shall have the right to terminate
this Lease as of the date on which such damage occurs, through written notice to the other party, to be given within fifteen (15) days after the occurrence of such damage;
except that should such damage or destruction occur as the result of the abuse or negligence of Tenant, or its invitees, then Owner only shall have the right to termination.
Should this right be exercised by either Owner or Tenant, then rent for the current month shall be prorated between the parties as of the date the damage occurred and any
prepaid rent and unused security deposit shall be refunded to Tenant. If this Lease is not terminated, then Owner shall promptly repair the premises and there shall be a
proportionate deduction of rent until the premises are repaired and ready for Tenant's occupancy. The proportionate reduction shall be based on the extent to which the
making or repairs interferes with Tenant's reasonable use of the premises.

ENTRY AND INSPECTION: Owner shall have the right to enter the premises: (a) in case of emergency; (b) to make necessary or agreed repairs, decorations, alterations,
improvements, supply necessary or agreed services, exhibit the premises to prospective or actual purchasers, mortgagees, tenants, workmen, or contractors; (c) when
tenant has abandoned or surrendered the premises. Except under (a) and (c), entry may not be made other than during normal business hours, and without not less than 24
hours prior notice to Tenant.

INDEMNIFICATION: Owner shall not be liable for any damage or injury to Tenant, or any other person, or to any property, occurring on the premises, or any part thereof, or
in common areas thereof, unless such damage is the proximate result of the negligence or unlawful act of Owner, his agents, or his employees. Tenant agrees to hold
Owner harmless from any claims for damages no matter how caused, except for injury or damages for which Owner is legally responsible.

POSSESSION: If Owner is unable to deliver possession of the premises at the commencement hereof, Owner shall not be liable for any damage caused thereby, nor shall
this agreement be void or voidable, but Tenant shall not be liable for any rent until possession is delivered. Tenant may terminate this agreement if possession is not

delivered within _____ days of the commencement of the term hereof.

DEFAULT: If Tenant shall fail to pay rent when due, or perform any term hereof, after not less than three (3) days written notice of such default given in the manner required
by law, the Owner, at his option, may terminate all rights of Tenant hereunder, unless Tenant, within said time, shall cure default. If Tenant abandons or vacates the
property, while in default of the payment of rent, Owner may consider any property left on the premises to be abandoned and may dispose of the same in any manner
allowed by law. In the event the Owner reasonably believes that such abandoned property has no value, it may be discarded. All property on the premises is hereby subject
to a lien in favor of Owner for the payment of all sums due hereunder, to the maximum extent allowed by law.

In the event of a default by Tenant, Owner may elect to (a) continue the lease in effect and enforce all his rights and remedies hereunder, including the right to recover
the rent as it becomes due, or (b) at any time, terminate all of Tenant's rights hereunder and recover from Tenant all damages he may incur by reason of the breach of the
lease, including the cost of recovering the premises, and including the worth at the time of such termination, or at the time of an award if suit be instituted to enforce this provision, of the amount by which the unpaid rent for the balance of the term exceeds the amount of such rent loss which the Tenant proves could be reasonably avoided.

Fig. 12-3. A residential lease/rental agreement.

SECURITY: The security deposit set forth, if any, shall secure the performance of Tenant's obligations hereunder. Owner may, but shall not be obligated to, apply all or portions of said deposit on account of Tenant's obligations hereunder. Any balance remaining upon termination shall be returned to Tenant. Tenant shall not have the right to apply the security deposit in payment of the last month's rent.

DEPOSIT REFUNDS: The balance of all deposits shall be refunded within two (2) weeks from date possession is delivered to Owner or his Authorized Agent, together with a statement showing any charges made against such deposits by Owner.

ATTORNEY'S FEES: In any legal action brought by either party to enforce the terms hereof or relating to the demised premises, the prevailing party shall be entitled to all costs incurred in connection with such action, including a reasonable attorney's fee.

WAIVER: No failure of Owner to enforce any term hereof shall be deemed a waiver. The acceptance of rent by Owner shall not waive his right to enforce any term hereof.

NOTICES: Any notice which either party may give, or is required to give, may be given by mailing the same, postage prepaid, to Tenant at the premises or to Owner at the address shown below or at such other places as may be designated by the parties from time to time.

HOLDING OVER: Any holding over after expiration hereof, with the consent of Owner, shall be construed as a month-to-month tenancy in accordance with the terms hereof, as applicable, until either party shall terminate the same by giving the other party thirty (30) days written notice delivered by certified mail.

TIME: Time is of the essence of this agreement.

□ **ADDITIONAL TERMS AND CONDITIONS** are set forth on page two.

ENTIRE AGREEMENT: The foregoing constitutes the entire agreement between the parties and may be modified only by a writing signed by both parties. The following Exhibits, if any, have been made a part of this agreement before the parties' execution hereof: _____

The undersigned Tenant hereby acknowledges receipt of a copy hereof.   DATED: _____

_____ Real Estate Company   _____ Tenant

By _____   _____

ACCEPTANCE: _____ Owner   _____ DATED: _____

ADDITIONAL TERMS AND CONDITIONS: _____
_____
_____
_____
_____

Tenant's Initials: (_____ _____)

Owner's Initials: (_____)

COMMISSION AGREEMENT

The Owner agrees to pay to _____ , the Broker in this transaction,

the sum of $ _____ for services rendered and authorizes Agent to deduct said sum from the deposit received from Tenant.

In the event the Lease is extended for a definite period of time or on a month-to-month basis after the expiration of the original term, Owner shall pay to Broker an additional commission of _____ percent (_____%) of the total rental for the extended period. This commission shall be due and payable at the commencement of the extended period if for a fixed term, or if on a month-to-month basis, at the termination of Tenant's occupancy or one year, whichever is earlier.

In the event a sale or exchange of the real property is made to Tenant or any member of Tenant's family during the occupancy of Tenant or within one hundred and eighty (180) calendar days after the termination of occupancy of Tenant, then Owner agrees to pay Broker a commission of _____ percent (_____%) of the sale price or exchange value. This agreement shall not limit the rights of Agent provided for in any listing or other agreement which may be in effect between Owner and Agent.

NOTICE: The amount or rate of real estate commissions is not fixed by law. They are set by each broker individually and may be negotiable between the owner and broker.

The undersigned Owner hereby acknowledges receipt of a copy hereof.   DATED: _____

_____ Owner's Authorized Agent   _____ Owner

_____ Address   _____ Phone

By _____

TENANT'S PERSONAL AND CREDIT INFORMATION

(In the event of co-tenants, other than spouses, use separate sheet for each tenant.)

		Social Security No.	
Name	Date of Birth	Drivers Lic. No.	Expir. Date
Name of Co-Tenant		Social Security No.	
Present Address		Driver Lic. No.	Expir. Date
City/State/Zip	Res. Phone	Bus. Phone	
How long at present address	Landlord or Agent	Phone	
Previous Address	How long	Landlord or Agent	Phone
City/State/Zip			
Occupants: Relationships: / Ages:		Pets?	
Car Make	Year	Model	Color	License No.

OCCUPATION

	PRESENT OCCUPATION*	PRIOR OCCUPATION*	CO-TENANT'S OCCUPATION
Occupation			
Employer			
Self-employed, d.b.a			
Business Address			
Business Phone			
Type of Business			
Position held			
Name and Title of Superior			
How long			
Monthly Gross Income			

*If employed or self-employed less than two years,
give same information on prior occupation.

REFERENCES

Bank Reference		Address		Phone	
CREDIT REFERENCE	ACCOUNT NO	ADDRESS	HIGHEST AMOUNT OWED	PURPOSE OF CREDIT	ACCOUNT OPEN OR DATE CLOSED
PERSONAL REFERENCE		ADDRESS	PHONE	LENGTH OF ACQUAINTANCE	OCCUPATION
NEAREST RELATIVE		ADDRESS	PHONE	CITY	RELATIONSHIP

Have you ever filed a petition of bankruptcy? _____ have you ever been evicted from any tenancy? _____

Have you ever wilfully and intentionally refused to pay any rent when due? _____

I DECLARE THAT THE FOREGOING IS TRUE AND CORRECT, AUTHORIZE ITS VERIFICATION AND THE OBTAINING OF A CREDIT REPORT.

I agree that Landlord may terminate any agreement entered into in reliance on any misstatement made above.   DATED: _____

_____ Applicant   _____ Applicant

13

Establish
a Sound
Credit and
Collection Policy

WE'VE ESTABLISHED THE FACT THAT THE TENANTS ARE THE LIFE BLOOD of the real estate business. The rent is the plasma that keeps the whole business alive. Without the rent—and it's a pretty obvious statement to make—the business would die.

Learning how to set a credit and collection policy is as important a phase of management as there is for the business to succeed. If you're new in the business or even if you've been in it for years, you need to learn everything there is to know about establishing this credit policy. Let's start.

SET A CREDIT POLICY

The credit policy is simple. The rent must be paid on time. If it's due on the first of the month, that's when it's due, and not on the fifth or tenth.

You might ask, "That all sounds well and good, but how do I know whether I'm going to get paid or not?" The next topic will answer that question.

JOIN A CREDIT BUREAU

There's only one surefire way to control the credit of any business and that is to know the history of how people pay their bills. There's only one way to find out this information and that is through a credit bureau.

Approximately 3,400 credit bureaus exist throughout the country, serving every urban and rural community. Consequently, within a short distance from your home, there's a bureau that can serve you. That bureau provides service to any and all businesses, including real estate investors. Whether you own 1 property or 100, the availability of this service is very important. Renters should know how their potential tenant pays his obligations.

The credit bureau service is reasonably simple and inexpensive. Check through the yellow pages, simply call the manager, introduce yourself, and tell him what kind of service you need. He'll tell you his membership and service dues.

Most bureaus provide a number of services, including reporting, check collecting, and collecting past-due accounts. The reporting service is immediately available by telephone, mail, or computer.

The credit record maintained by the bureau consists of the pay records of the individual or business, including local ratings as well as national. The file includes all credit cards, bank loans, department store accounts, real estate loans, and student loans. It also includes judgments and bankruptcies, as well as accounts for collection turned over to the credit bureau. Incidentally, only a credit bureau can record and report accounts for collection on an individual.

This entire file gives a complete history of the paying habits of the individual. It's the kind of information that can and will help you determine whether you want the individual as a tenant and how he is going to pay you.

Membership in a credit bureau isn't difficult or expensive. Most bureaus charge about $120 per year for membership and about $2.50 per report.

Think of it this way: If you save one bad risk, you'll have paid your membership fee for one year. Not only that, but if you know your tenant is a good credit risk and you are assured of being paid, you will have peace of mind.

USE THE INFORMATION FOR YOUR OWN PROTECTION

It's just as important to use the information as it is to get it. Here's what I mean.

If that person has a history of not paying his bills—whether it's a drug store, doctor, or whatever—he's not going to pay you either.

I know people who think they've got a certain something and, despite the bad credit record, that person's going to pay them. There's the other real estate investor who wants to fill that vacancy no matter what. He knows the perspective tenant has bad credit, but after all, he's Joe Nice Guy and the tenant certainly isn't going to cheat him.

Also, there are times when we let greed get in our way—especially in the way of common sense. We receive the negative information about the individual but won't believe it.

All these things constitute bad risks and eventually bad accounts that must be turned over the collection. So, get the information and operate your business with common sense. Reject the tenants that don't pay.

ENFORCE YOUR RENT POLICY

Setting the credit policy isn't all that difficult. Let the tenant know you appreciate him as a tenant, but also that you've got to be paid in order to keep the apartment going.

If you've set the policy that the rent is due on the first and the tenant gets behind, there's nothing wrong with asking for your money. This request can certainly be done in a friendly and businesslike manner, without upsetting the tenant.

At one time or another, you're going to have a tenant come to you and ask, "I'm short this month and just don't have the money to pay the rent. Can you wait?" or "I had to make a car payment and I don't have the money." or "My daughter went to the dentist and now I'm short." If the tenant is recently divorced, you can hear something like this, "My children came to visit me and I had to pay their transportation."

These questions are stall tactics. Make up your mind that you don't do business on this basis. My theory is this: the tenant's concerns should be: food, housing, utilities, and all other expenses—in that order.

In the stall tactic, the first thing to do is call to their attention the fact that food and housing should be their first priority. Then tell them you aren't in the loan business.

For the younger tenant, I'll usually let them know that I, as the landlord, don't have any family obligation to them to provide them with housing, a loan, or anything else. That's their own family's responsibility and they should go to their parents and get help.

After all, you rent apartments and expect to be paid when the rent comes due. You're not playing second fiddle to a car payment or some other excuse. Tell them to go to a relative, friend, employer, or anyone else and get their financial help.

I also let that tenant know I have a mortgage payment that has to be paid with the rent money, and the bank won't wait.

Being assertive usually gets results. I've found that once I set them straight on this policy, it usually doesn't happen again.

EYE-BALLING CREDIT POLICY DOESN'T WORK

I know people in the business who can't turn down a tenant. They say, "He sure looks good to me and I know I'm going to get paid." So they take him on simply by looks—no other credit control. It's what I call *eye-balling*—looking at the person and saying he's good.

Eye-balling credit managers are operating in every business. I can assure you, it doesn't work. Anyone doing it is doomed to lose money.

HINDSIGHT CREDIT CHECKING DOESN'T WORK

There's the real estate investor who'll approve the tenant on the spot then go back to the office and call for a credit report. This system is just as bad as eye-balling and it doesn't work either. The collection departments of credit bureaus are filled with accounts like these. Check first.

IF THEY DON'T PAY, YOU DON'T WANT THEM

Let's say you have a tenant in one of your apartments that's not paying their rent. Obviously you're losing money and it's as bad or worse than having a vacancy. Therefore, the first step is to correct this situation before it gets out of hand. It's a case of either getting paid or getting rid of the tenant. You're not obligated to provide *free* housing to anyone, and not being paid rent is free housing.

The last thing in the world you need, especially the beginning investor, is an occupied apartment that isn't earning any money. The payment has to be met, the expenses don't wait, so the rent has to be there. Therefore, make up your mind that you're in the real estate business for one thing, and that is to make a profit. In order to make a profit it takes money. The only way to get the money is collect the rents—on time.

WHAT TO DO WITH AN
OCCUPIED APARTMENT NOT EARNING RENT

Several ways exist to address the problem of an occupied apartment not earning any money.

This shouldn't happen, in the first place, if there has been a concerted effort in checking the tenant before they move into the apartment. Let's say this is a case where the tenant checked out good and then turned bad and isn't paying.

First, analyze the situation. Is the tenant working full-time? Does the tenant have enough money that they should be able to pay the rent? Or, does it appear that they're spending rent money for other things?

The next thing is to confront the tenant *very* assertively about the problem. If it appears once the problem is worked out, that the tenant will eventually be good and live up to the rental agreement, then discuss ways of getting the thing straightened out. Straightened out means getting your money. It's a matter of letting that tenant know what he should consider to be his priorities. Let the tenant know, again very assertively, that you won't be low man on the totem pole of priorities. Rent always comes on the top side.

These decisions, during that crucial period of time, have to be made quickly. That's why it's important to remain assertive. This time is not the time to take a maybe or a stall answer. The money has to be produced here and now because any further stall only means an occupied apartment and still no money. Insist on that tenant getting the money—beg, borrow, steal, or whatever it takes, but you have to get paid, and there's no two ways about it. A stall is not an answer to the problem. Don't even consider stalls as excuses.

If this doesn't work, the next step is eviction. Eviction is truly one of the real headaches of the business. However, it doesn't happen that often, especially if the tenant is checked out thoroughly before entering into the apartment lease.

HOW TO GET RID OF THE NONPAYERS

Now let's say you have a tenant who isn't paying. I don't mean they're 10 or 15 days late, I mean they're socked into the apartment and haven't paid for a month or two. What's next?

There's only one way to get that apartment back in the profit picture and that's by eliminating the problem—the nonpaying tenant. Getting rid of that nonpaying tenant is called *eviction*.

Many legal ramifications exist in evicting a tenant. Each state has specific laws which spell out how it can be done. As far as I'm concerned, there's only one way—hire an attorney. Don't try to evict legally without legal advice.

I've told you before, I've been in this business for 25 years. During that time I've evicted tenants and, have to tell you, I've done it without legal aid. Here's how that can work for you.

First of all, 99 percent of the time the tenant knows he is wrong. When he realizes he is wrong, it's impossible for him to hide from the raw truth. Hence, we deal with the truth.

The truth is that eviction by legal means becomes an embarrassing experience for that tenant. The truth also is that they don't want their "dirty baggage" brought out in the public courts.

Let's take a look at what constitutes that "dirty baggage":

- Property damage
- Poor housekeeping
- Loud parties

- Uncontrolled drinking
- Violence
- Abusive language
- Tenant and neighbor complaints
- Late hours
- Unkept premises
- Loud and dangerous pets
- Fights and rowdiness
- Nonpayment of rent

Never enter a tenant's apartment without their authority to do so. *Do not* lock the tenant out of their apartment nor confiscate his or her property in lieu of past due rent. Do not forcefully enter a tenant's premises without legal authority to do so.

If the "dirty baggage" is presented correctly by the owner, that tenant can save face. First, have a confrontation and present the complaint and problem. Next, by being *extremely assertive*, let that tenant know you want him out, and out *right now!* At this stage, how assertive you are will make the difference of what happens next.

Now you know you have their attention. Usually when that individual is confronted with the truth and knows he is in the wrong, he won't put up much of a fight, if any at all. He oftentimes becomes very humble, gives in, and knows he can't win. In this case, don't give in and don't back down. Don't change your mind if you see tears in his eyes. If you give in, accept him back, you're going to have the same problem, maybe in a month or two, despite all their promises.

If you become wishy-washy, you'll end up a loser and the tenant will take advantage of you and literally walk all over you. He doesn't have much to lose if he thinks he can overcome you. If you let him move back in, it will be costly and possibly you will have legal problems—something any property owner can do without.

PROTECT YOURSELF AGAINST LEGAL ACTION

When you're involved with any potential legal problem attributed to any dispute with your property, my advice is:

- Contact an attorney
- Keep precise records and details

Keep a daily log, right from the first communication and keep all the following information:

- Time, date, and communication at time of confrontation
- Reasons for confrontation
- Chronological order of events including dates and times
- A record of all conversation involving the dispute
- Names of others involved in dispute

I can assure you that if you do end up in court, these records will speak louder than words. The landlord has a tough time dealing with the court system anyway. Some judges think all people who own apartments or rental property are rich and selfish. In most cases that judge will look at the case of the "rich landlord" vs. the "poor tenant". Your good records sometimes are the only way to combat this case.

Good records are a valuable asset in all real estate transactions. Prepare yourself for any unusual or unforeseen circumstances at all times.

If you've ever been to court you know that a good, well-prepared case will win. Usually the defendant will end up being caught in a lie. When you show up with the dates, times and conversations that have taken place, the judge knows you're not trying to pull one over on the tenant. Maybe this situation is something that you'll never have to encounter, but it's something that can happen at any time.

Whatever you do, don't use threats. Don't be abusive, don't use foul language, and don't do anything illegal.

HOW TO COLLECT PAST-DUE RENT

One last item should be talked about in the credit collection business when operating a profitable real estate business. That is, collecting past-due rent.

Despite all our well-laid plans, we can, on occasion, get stuck with past-due rent. If this happens, don't sit on them. The longer you don't pay attention, the bigger the loss. Let me give you an example of what I mean.

- $100 paid on time is worth $100
- $100 past due 60 days is worth $90
- $100 past due 6 months is worth $67
- $100 past due one year is worth $45

Nothing is worse than having to write-off a bad debt. It's something that makes most of us boil. Therefore, if you end up with a bad debt, take every conceivable action necessary to get your money. Being nice isn't going to get a penny. In fact, being nice only leads to more trouble and more loss.

Start your collection efforts by contacting the person who owes you the money and tell them, "My accountant (banker, wife, anyone) told me I have to get this money collected because if I don't, I'll be past due on my payments." You can even say, "If I don't get this money, I'm in trouble and I've been ordered to collect or else."

Again, it's time to be assertive. Let them know you mean business; keep the pressure on for the payment. Call frequently and demand payment. If you don't make progress after a short period of time the next step is to use a bill collector.

The Bill Collector

Get this bad debt over with so you can get yourself back to the positive things happening with your real estate. Work with the good tenants and your good property. Don't waste time and effort, get burned out, and then get sick and tired of the whole thing.

Turn the bad debt over to a credit bureau of your choice for collection. If you use a credit bureau, that account for collection will appear on the debtor's credit file. There's some satisfaction in knowing you'll have an affect on that record.

If the credit bureau is good they'll get your money. This collection assistance can cost anywhere from 33 percent to 50 percent.

Legal Means of Collection

You can, of course, use an attorney and take legal measures to collect the past-due account. However, I've found that most attorneys don't like to handle these small accounts.

If your debtor has contacted an attorney to represent him, it's my understanding you have to cease all communications with the debtor and communicate only through your attorney and his attorney. However, don't take any abuse from the attorney if you're in the right. And, don't take a settlement.

Another method of taking legal action is through conciliation court or small claims court. Here's the way that works. Conciliation court was established so anyone can file a complaint without having an attorney involved. You pay a fee to file in the court; the hearing is held before a judge. He rules that you're right or the debtor is right. If you're right, you get a judgement.

Conciliation court doesn't collect the money. Therefore, you have to follow through once the judgement is issued and there are some legal ramifications involved. In fact, it's usually more trouble than it's worth.

I personally have used a credit bureau and they've filed in conciliation court.

14

Dealing with Tenant Complaints, Problems, and Rents

Up to this point, the only investment you've had to make to this substantial savings account is a small down payment. The tenant's rent pays your mortgage each month. If the rent money keeps coming in—other people's money—then your contribution, that of management, should be easy.

Good management practices can help you avoid a lot of problems. If you're serious about investing in real estate, then take the time to learn the business and take care of the property. If not, it can mean disaster. Here's an example of what I mean.

Remember I told you about an investor who bought 10 rental units. He did a great job for the first four to five years. Then he got lax and careless about taking care of the property. He let things get run-down, didn't mow the lawns, didn't paint, and neglected the tenant's complaints. Eventually the good tenants moved out, the money quit flowing, and an avalanche of trouble began. As the problems piled up, he lost interest and began treating the property with disdain.

Next the properties turned into slums. There were persistent vacancies and the tenants living there didn't pay their rent. The entire operation got out of hand and the last I heard, he was going to let the property go back on foreclosure.

YOUR TENANTS ARE YOUR BUSINESS

Remember, I said tenants expect their apartment to be treated as a serious business. Part of that seriousness involves making a special effort to be a good landlord. This effort can and will pay off. By developing this reputation, it can enhance your ability to choose and select the best tenants.

Being a good landlord doesn't mean you must cater to every whim and wish of every tenant. It's a matter of caring for the legitimate problems. The point is, don't let the little things get out of hand. Fix the leaky faucet, plugged drain, torn carpet, and those things that are irritating.

Let the tenants know you're concerned about them as individuals and that you really do care about them and their apartment. Remember, this apartment is their home and they want to keep it as nice as possible.

When confronting tenants and their problems, avoid arguments. They only create bad feelings and more problems. You can do without these. Work out their complaints together, however, don't let them take advantage of you. If you do, they'll chase you to death with their requests.

If you've done a good job of screening your tenants, you should be getting the best. If they're the best, they should have your respect and consideration.

TAKE ADVANTAGE OF COMPLAINTS

Turn tenant's complaints into a positive event. Here's an opportunity to relate directly with them. If you give good service, they'll go away feeling good and, chances are they'll remain devoted and loyal as a tenant. Remember too, good relationships make you feel good.

Service adds that special touch. It's that extra effort that is important—doing something that's totally unexpected. Service doesn't take a lot of time, very little effort, and practically no money.

Service is something that's positive and the returns are usually manyfold, especially if the word gets out that you're a service oriented landlord. The word will get out; this fact will add to your ability to get and keep the best of tenants.

SOLVING PROBLEMS AND COMPLAINTS

No matter how many units, no matter how new and well-kept the apartments are, there will be problems. You can, and will, get calls for any of the following, just about anytime:

- Lost key to apartment
- Hall lights burned out
- Plugged sewer

- Leaky roof
- Door won't open or close
- Window won't open or close
- Broken door lock
- Leaky faucet or shower
- Washing machine or dryer out of order
- No heat
- Water leaking through ceiling
- Freezer defrosting when it shouldn't
- Stove burner doesn't heat
- Carpet is dirty
- Apartment needs painting
- Sewer backed up in basement
- Refrigerator doesn't cool
- Bathtub doesn't drain
- Kitchen sink won't drain
  etc.

Three categories of complaints exist. Each should be treated differently. Let's take a look

- Catastrophic: This category can be a backed-up sewer, water in the basement, roof leaking, heating system out of order, etc. These demand *immediate attention*.
- Money-savers: Covers leaky faucets, coin-operated washer/dryer not working, hall lights too bright, etc. Take care of these as soon as possible.
- All others: Painting, carpet cleaning, etc., are all things that can be done on weekends with no urgency.

When a tenant calls with a complaint, be sure it gets attention right away so that a small problem doesn't turn into a catastrophe.

THE ART OF ELIMINATING COMPLAINTS

First, consider hiring one of the tenants to look after the building and grounds. When I say hire, it's like before, charge less rent so there's no payroll. This way all the complaints go directly to the manager with the understanding that you, the owner, get called in an emergency situation.

When you are dealing with persistent complainers, and you will, let them know in a firm manner that you can't be running all the time over nitty-gritty problems. Once you show the tenant you mean business, eventually they'll quit calling. Some of them figure it's a lot easier to get the problem fixed themselves rather than going through the hassle of dealing with an assertive manager.

When you do have a persistent complainer that you can't satisfy, tell them, "Maybe you'd be happier renting from someone else or in another apartment." They either quit complaining or move. Either way, you're better off.

COMMON-SENSE RENT CONTROL MEANS MORE INCOME

There is no prescribed way to determine rents. Rents are based on whatever the traffic will bear. This concept is better known as supply and demand.

Each apartment and rental unit must contribute to sound economic sense; otherwise, why bother to invest in real estate. If you're not charging enough rent, there's no reason to buy the property. Put the money in CD's.

Your main concern is to know your market. For instance, if vacancies in the community do not exist it's a seller's market and you can charge accordingly.

On the other hand, if vacancies do exist you might have to drop the amount of rent for each apartment. It's better to charge $10 to $25 a month less on rent rather than having a vacancy.

Here's something to think about when setting fair rents. Ask yourself, "If I rented my apartment, would I be satisfied with the rent?"

Another way to determine what rent to charge is check with the neighbors, especially the large apartment units. Once you know their prices and know what kind of property or apartment they have, you can establish your rent accordingly.

Incidentally, as you see the large apartment unit owners raising rents, it's a good time to analyze your rents. Also, visit with your fellow investors, especially the small operators. Keep in touch with how much they charge then you will have some idea of what your apartments are worth.

WHEN TO RAISE RENTS

You are justified to raise rents at certain times. For instance, most tenants, especially government employees and social security recipients, receive annual cost-of-living increases. This cost of living means housing. It's a time to consider raising rents.

Inflation comes natural. With inflation comes an increase in rents. Raise rents when there's an increase in taxes.

The easiest time to raise rents is at a time of vacancy. If the market will bear it, increase the rent each time a tenant moves out.

BEING OVERLY CONSIDERATE
OF THE TENANT CAN BE COSTLY

Sometimes we small investors let our emotions get involved in our business transactions and we lose sight of why we're in business. This fact is especially true when it comes to charging rents.

Many times I've heard landlords say, "Oh, they're such a nice couple I hate to raise their rent, " or "She's such a nice old lady, never demands anything, is on social security, and I just don't feel right charging any more rent."

Now all that's well and good, but remember you're not in the rental business to make friends, be a nice guy, and consider this a part of your civic duty. If you want to be a do-gooder be a boy scout leader or collect for your community chest. Don't do it with your real estate business. You're in that business for profit.

Charging too little rent and not raising rents when they should be raised is futile and foolhardy. It might be considered nice, but it certainly doesn't make business sense and won't add a penny to the bank account.

We talked about that nice old lady or couple that rents from you, and it's just not right to raise their rent. The odds are pretty good that most of these people have a pretty hefty savings account. I'd be willing to bet that once they leave the apartment, Joe Nice Guy Landlord might be quickly forgotten. You might have thought you were really doing a good deed, but do you think for one minute these tenant's heirs are going to sit there in the attorney's office settling the estate and say, "Oh that wonderful Joe Nice Guy Landlord. He was such a good person to have taken care of my mother. I think we should let him in on some of the inheritance."

Hah! Those heirs will be grubbing for every penny they can get. All those years Joe Nice Guy didn't charge enough rent are up in flames.

If you feel compelled to give your money away, then give it to your children, not your tenants.

CHARGE THE PROPER RENT

I knew a real estate investor who had the greatest reputation with his tenants. He never raised his rents. For this reason every tenant thought he was such a great guy and they also said nice flattering things about him. I told him he couldn't put those nice words in the bank.

I'm not advocating that it's necessary to be obnoxious; it's just a matter of using common sense and charging the rent that fits the apartment, not the person. As a matter of fact, it's just as easy to be a nice guy and charge the correct rent also.

Having a lackadaisical attitude about charging proper rents means you're probably not making good sound business and financial judgements. I don't think anyone can accuse you of standing on the street corner and handing out dollar bills. Well, not charging enough rent is giving away your money.

DISPEL THE CADILLAC IMAGE WITH YOUR TENANTS

I don't think it's a good idea to drive up to your apartments, in front of your tenants, in a big status symbol car. If you do, I think you're asking for trouble. It seems to me you're going to get a negative reaction. For example, someone might say, ''This guy's making big bucks if he can afford that kind of car. He must be charging too much rent and rippin' us off.''

I'd recommend going to the apartments in casual clothing, an older car, and make it look like you're one of them and that you can't afford anything better. After all, these people are living in apartments most likely because they're not wealthy. In addition, do your own work and give the tenants the impression that you can't afford to hire it done.

THE MEANING OF TENANT LEASES

For the most part, a lease doesn't hold a lot of water. For instance, if your tenant's going to move out in the middle of a lease, they're moving because they have too. However, it can protect you against past-due rent, clean up, fix up and repairs.

A whole book could be written on drawing up leases. I'd recommend you check with an attorney or find an already written lease you can incorporate into your business.

15

A Good
Mental Attitude
Enhances Success

IN THIS CHAPTER I'D LIKE TO COVER SOME "LEFTOVER" TOPICS WHICH weren't discussed in the previous chapters. These leftovers make a difference in the total operation of any real estate project.

Most of these leftovers have to do with your own personal input into the business. For example, success can depend heavily on you maintaining the following personal characteristics:

- Having a good mental attitude
- Thinking positive about yourself and the business
- Being highly motivated
- Eliminating the negative aspects in your life
- Developing leadership abilities
- Having the ability to make precise decisions
- Ability to overcome fears
- Avoiding real estate burnout

Let's take a look at each one of these characteristics and see what affect they can have on the overall picture of real estate investing. None of these characteristics are so profound or difficult to acquire that they can't be easily nurtured and developed to enhance the business operation. Let's take a look.

A GOOD MENTAL ATTITUDE PAYS IN EVERY WAY

Whether you're in the real estate business or any other business, it doesn't take a Norman Vincent Peale to tell you that having a positive mental and emotional attitude about yourself and your business can and will contribute to your well-being, make life easier, save money, time, and effort, and, add to your peace of mind.

That's a lot to say. To cover it more briefly, here's an answer to the following question I'm often asked, "What single thing can I do to make sure my business becomes successful and secure?" The answer is, "Think positive!"

Thinking positive, acting positive, and being positive is the least expensive investment anyone can make to their business or even to their everyday living. When it comes to real estate, it's not difficult to think positive, because the truth is, real estate itself is positive.

THE FUTURE IN REAL ESTATE IS POSITIVE

Times have never been better for investing in real estate. I'm thoroughly convinced that with a little more than average intelligence and ambition, a good attitude, and some positive motivation, there's no end to what can be done in the real estate business.

You're probably saying about now, "Here we go again, with all these highfalutin ideas. How does he think they can work for me?" Although I'm not a professional motivator, I think I can get you going. Here's how.

Form the Habit of Positive Thinking

The *mind*, and only the *mind*, determines how we think and feel and act. Therefore, it's a matter of training the mind correctly. The correct way is to think positive all the time.

There's only one individual who can control your mind and how it thinks each day. That person is you!

Think of it this way. We have a very simple choice each day when we get up. We can start the day however we wish. The way in which we set our mind in action at the beginning of the day carries us throughout the day. Start with something negative and most likely the day will end up negative. Begin the day with a positive attitude and it will end positive.

If we accept the fact that we have this choice, and that it doesn't take any extra effort, time, or energy to make this choice then it's important we make the right choice. Why not start each day with a bright, beaming, positive attitude?

If you meet and greet your peer group each day with a positive attitude, this attitude can and will carry over to them. Pretty soon everyone around you will feel good. You can and will develop power with other people because they'll want to be around you. Most people like doing business with those who are cheerful, optimistic, and positive. Tenants like having a positive landlord.

Not only is your positive attitude good for business but it also plays a dramatic role in your entire life. The positive and confident attitude is good for the body and soul. Besides business success and a better emotional state of mind, happy, positive people are healthier. This fact alone is such a great attribute of thinking, acting, and being positive.

Here's another item to add to the unlimited list of benefits of positive thinking. Positive people are successful people, who seem to have 100 percent control over their abilities, creativity, and productivity. They seem to produce more in thought and work—all the time.

Some of us seem to get by using about 50 percent or 60 percent of our abilities. This fact usually contributes to laziness and puts us in the category of nondoers, procrastinators, and nonowners.

Set Up a Positive Atmosphere All Around You

Part of this overall plan of developing a positive attitude is surround yourself with positive people, including your family. Develop and nurture good positive communications with your mate and family. Universally I've found that family plays an important part in most people's lives. Therefore, make sure the family environment is such that it adds brightness to your life.

Make sure all those around you have a vocabulary that includes good fortune, prosperity, success, accomplishment, victory, and winning.

Set the Plan of Positivism in Action Now

Most of what I've had to offer is simple, and as I said before, doesn't take much time, effort, or energy. With the right state of mind these ideas can be utilized daily. None of them are difficult and certainly don't cost anything. It proves the best things in life are free.

It's just as easy to start the day with a positive plan and work on it perpetually. Eventually it can, and will, be a habit. Like the real estate business itself, you have to start now.

MOTIVATION CREATES MONEY, INCOME, AND PROFITS

Let's see where positivism can take us. One thing for certain, positivism is a built-in motivator.

Any investor will tell you they're motivated by real estate because it produces financial rewards. In fact, there's no greater motivator than profit. But to be motivated to make profit takes some extra special effort. That effort is called enthusiasm.

Positivism isn't the sum total of the successful real estate investor, but it certainly is a major contributing factor to his success.

I'm not a professional motivator, and I don't have all the answers on how to get you "up" and going, but I've got some ideas that might work.

First of all, get yourself in "gear" and get going. Only you can do that. I can't get up with you each morning and give you a pep talk. My message right here and now is, like any other motivator, temporary and fleeting. It's entirely up to you to get yourself going. Once you take that step, it's just as important that you don't slip back. Don't let it be a temporary action, and then lose interest, and slip back into the old habits—that of negativism and an I don't care attitude.

Unless there's some effort initiated, we do in fact slip back and get into the old rut. Don't let this happen to you. If you've read this book up to now, and you're getting excited about your future, keep it up.

The golden ring of opportunity is there to be had. Someone grabs it everyday of the week. There's no reason anyone of us can't do the same thing.

Let's look at Webster's definition of positive:

. . . directed or moving toward a source of stimulation. Fully assured, confident, incontestable, unqualified.

You might ask yourself, "Is this the way I carry on my daily activities—positive, moving forward, both on a personal as well as a business basis?" or, "Do I have some negative elements that have taken over my life and have encroached on my thinking?" Let's take a look at eliminating the negative attitude.

NEGATIVISM DOESN'T WORK

Look around you. Some people you meet everyday are complaining knifing, rumor-mongering, and very dull. They add nothing to life and only drag everyone down around them. Avoid them.

The movers and shakers, the positive people, those who control most of our economy, are all doing pretty well and, in general, are making mone~ ... ~ie seem to have things running pretty smoothly and ~ ..ssrully. Almost daily we hear about another new millionaire that's ..iade it in the real estate business. That's positive.

On the other hand, about 10 percent of the businesses, including real estate investors, are having a tough time. As we've illustrated before, most of this trouble and the tough times are self-inflicted through mismanagement, greed, overspending and oftentimes, having too big an ego to fill.

You know these people. Some of them we see personally every day; some of them we see in the news every day. You might work with a lot of them.

I can't help them. But maybe my humble advice might keep you from getting into this trap. My advice is simply this. Stay away from losers. They'll drag you down. In fact, a lot of these types don't have a good self-esteem and they have a need to drag others down to their level. They can't stand to be around success or successful people.

If somebody's going broke in business let it be the other guy—don't let it happen to you.

These negative people have always been around us. Historically, there have been about 10 percent of the businesses who are in financial trouble for one reason or another. That percentage hasn't changed dramatically for years. Oh, I agree, back in the depression there were a lot more failures, but in the past four to five decades there hasn't been a great change. The only difference is that we have a communication system that seems to dwell on the negative aspect and that's what we read and hear.

Let me give you an idea of what I mean. We get messages like,

- Consumer debt loan
- Depressed farm economy
- Recession
- Depression

Here's a comment from a recent news article:

. . . with so many problems and situations developing at one point in time the recession could be severe.

That writer and all these messages are wrong and do nothing but create negativism, anxieties, and fear.

The daily news reporters spew out negative news reports and by the time it's over, we think the world's coming to an end, that every business in the nation is failing, our economy is going under, and we're heading for a depression. I've heard this for the past 30 years. It never changes. The problem is that these communicators have taken charge of our thinking. Common-sense thinking goes right out the window.

My advice then is, *don't* let this type information get to you. It's gobble de gook. If we listen to this information long enough, we'll cease business expansion, withdraw creativity and innovativeness, and we'll quit growing. I'm convinced that if we listen to the media reports long enough, we (the entire nation) could plunge into a depression. Don't let yourself get caught in this trap.

I can assure you of one thing about negativism, and that is, if you let these negative stories and reports get in your way, and if you associate with negative people, the chances are you'll remain negative and mediocre.

These anxieties created from a constant barrage of negativism will destroy you emotionally and drag you down. When you're down, it's difficult to get back up. Also, when you're down, business starts sliding. Pretty soon there are more anxieties because problems and complaints are neglected. This starts an anxiety-filled sinkhole.

By all means, eliminate the negative because it over-shadows the positive. When this happens, it's easy to let the *golden opportunity* pass you by.

Think, act, dream, and live positive.

STRONG LEADERSHIP CAN ENSURE SUCCESS

The next step is to develop and nurture your leadership abilities. All of us have leadership abilities, it's just that some of us ignore them.

Success comes by using a combination of ingredients—leadership, courage, and plain old guts. This combination has created within our system the ability for any of us to rise to the top. Those with the intestinal fortitude have surged ahead and reaped the harvest and gained the rewards.

Rewards in real estate, like any other business, come to that individual who takes the bull by the horns and gets things done, buys the real estate, and becomes successful.

The point is, it does take guts. You might ask yourself, "Do I have the ability to take on the management of real estate?" When you look for the answer to that question, keep in mind that it means handling the following:

- Tenant complaints

- Cleaning and caring for the property
- Nitty-gritty everyday service problems
- Periodic renovation work
- Fixing and repairing

or any number of things we've covered throughout this book.

I have a feeling if you've gotten this far in the book, you're pretty sure of yourself, quite motivated, and probably saying right about now, "You bet I can handle real estate and I'm going to get going—right now."

That's great, but make certain it's not just temporary. Three to four years down the line you'll still need that positive attitude, along with strong leadership, to keep the business going. It takes about that much time for the real estate honeymoon to be over.

If you stick with it, by then you should enjoy the rewards and see the progress. You'll recognize the solid, secure savings account you've developed, and you can observe how your work effort and time spent has paid off. Or, you might be sick and tired of the whole thing.

DECISION-MAKERS GET THINGS DONE

We've mentioned decision-making before in the book, but let's take one more look. Start by asking yourself, "Am I the type person who has the ability to make decisions, or do I follow decision-makers?"

In the real estate business, especially the small investors, you, and only you, have to make the decision. No committees, no department heads, no executives, and no managers exist to make the decision for you. It's entirely up to you.

Don't Complicate Decision-making

I read a book recently which said you have to do the following in order to make decisions:

- Diagnose the problem
- Diagram the problem
- Prepare pertinent information
- Have alternative solutions
- Check the criteria
- Translate the information
- Check the technique of probabilities
- Know the statistics and mathematical probabilities
- Check the computer information

This list sounds like a list from an individual who's never been under pressure to make a decision. Frankly, for the small investor, it's too much to comprehend and digest. It makes decisions difficult.

The point is, if decision-making becomes too complicated and too much of a problem, if we have to meet and confer, and if you have to go through a lot of rigamaroe, then decision-making becomes a chore.

Make the Decision and Live with It

Obviously, common sense tells you that you're not going to enter into a business proposition blindly. It's also obvious, when we reach the point of having to make that decision, whether it's buying more property or renovating property and selling it, we've done our own research and know what we're doing.

To make a decision takes some courage, a little practice, but more than anything else, a lot of common sense. I might add that a little instinct can help.

The main thing is make the decision. Don't procrastinate by saying, "Well, maybe I shouldn't..." or "It's alright, but..." Procrastination only slows things down and creates many anxieties. Then it becomes a "Catch 22" and another sinkhole.

What it comes down to is a matter of making the decision, right or wrong, and living with it. If it's wrong, don't fret, things will work themselves out, especially in real estate.

Time is one of the greatest assets of the real estate investor.

With every small business, including real estate, there are some risks. If we use common sense, however, for the most part, we'll be successful.

OVERCOME FEARS

Probably the major reason we procrastinate is because of fear. There's some justification for having some fears. It's a known fact that of all the new businesses which start in this country each year, only about one half of them survive for only two years, one third survive four years, and one fifth are owned by the founder at the end of ten years. In addition, we see record bankruptcies and business failures.

But these facts and statistics shouldn't place us in a position where we don't want to make a decision. There should be concern for fear, but not to the point of putting everything on hold and doing nothing. Once again, it's using common sense and knowing what you're doing, and the decisions become easy.

One more thought. If something emerges that creates fear, face whatever it is immediately. Don't put it off; this procrastination will only create anxiety. The longer the fear lasts, the more anxieties that are created—hence, a sinkhole.

DON'T MAKE YOUR WORK DIFFICULT

Sometimes we do get sick and tired of the daily chores of taking care of real estate. Pretty soon it's easy to build a mental block about the work and do nothing about it at all.

If you've got real estate work to do, do it. Get it organized; start with one task at a time and get it done. Don't take a look at all the work and think it's too much; then nothing get's done.

AVOID PHYSICAL AND EMOTIONAL BURNOUT

Some of the menial tasks can get tiresome. When this happens there can be burnout, or more simply put, you just get sick and tired of the business and the work. It can happen to anyone.

Once burnout sets in, the jobs aren't done and management tasks are overlooked. The property is ignored and the problems not only remain unsolved, but grow.

Burnout causes laziness and with laziness, things don't get done. Pretty soon weeds are growing in the lawn, broken doors or windows aren't fixed, the buildings aren't' painted, and there's a general deterioration of the property.

The next step is the good tenants become uninterested in the property, they move out, then vacancies occur. The property begins to decrease in value, the rents are gone, and you talk about a sinkhole, that's it!

Does all this sound unreasonable? It's not. It can happen, and does happen. Once the enthusiasm is gone and real estate investment becomes routine, it's easy to slip into complacency. Don't let it happen to you.

16

Cash In on the
Fruits of Your Labor

WE'RE GETTING CLOSE TO THE END NOW AND I DON'T WANT YOU TO LOSE sight of what this book is all about. For that reason we'll give a resume of what's been said.

There might be some repetition in this final summary, but the information and messages that are repeated are important enough that they should be said again.

Let's take a look at the finishing touches, the last hurrah, discover again the overwhelming benefits of owning investment real estate and then see how these benefits can improve our lives. This resume will be a positive review of real estate investing, just like real estate itself.

THE REAL ESTATE BUSINESS IS FOR EVERYONE

The most important message of this book is: *Real estate investing is one of the best, if not the only, ways in our free enterprise system, where the average, ordinary, common person, just like you and me, can build solid security and where that security can provide ways to enjoy the good things in life.*

There's hardly any other business where the common man can acquire wealth and build a secure future. Most of the other investments, businesses, or professions take either special education, a lot of capital, or a lifetime of work. Even with all that, there's no assurance of success.

REAL ESTATE IS A HEDGE AGAINST INFLATION

Even if we could make money and save it, inflation can dig deep into a savings account. This situation isn't the case with real estate because real estate is usually the first thing that increases in value during inflationary times.

For instance, did you know that from 1970 to 1980 general overall inflation was 6.8 percent? During that same time real estate inflated 9.4 percent. Inflation will continue, and all you have to do is look at the proof. For example, remember when an average home cost $18,000 to $20,000?

REAL ESTATE APPRECIATION IS A GIFT

Appreciation above all is one of the greatest financial benefits of real estate investing. It's a money-maker and, most of the time, earns without any effort, time, or money.

Appreciation comes with time. As we've said before, *time* is one of the greatest benefactors of the real estate business. You can buy real estate, manage it with competence, and sit back and watch it grow and appreciate. As a matter of fact, real estate grows regardless of what you do. This growth takes place in good times as well as bad. I see nothing in the foreseeable future that's going to change this. It's an ongoing occurrence and almost perpetual.

APPRECIATION THROUGH
PROPERTY AND COMMUNITY GROWTH

Improvement of property, repairing, rejuvenating, and fixing up increases the value of property. That same improvement not only increases the value but also increases the cash flow. As the property is improved, rents are increased.

A growing community will create financial growth in real estate within itself. However, there's one consideration that should be called to your attention, and that is when to know if a community is saturated with rentals.

To find the answer takes some investigative work. This work can be done by checking with other investors. Find out what the vacancy factor is in the community.

As an investor, the last thing you need is to buy in a community where the market is saturated with apartments and you end up with vacancies.

What I've found to counteract this saturation, is buy small one- and two-bedroom units in the medium price range. This technique is especially so of the older well-kept apartment units. Make certain they don't get rundown because, once they do, they'll no longer attract good tenants.

The nice thing about these older units is that the rents are less than the high-priced apartment complexes. There's a wide open market for this kind of apartment. In addition, if necessary, it's a lot easier to lower rents in the medium priced units. Although I can add, in all my years of real estate investing, never once have I had to lower rents.

REAL ESTATE INVESTORS USE OTHER PEOPLE'S MONEY

For an investment in real estate it takes little more than enough money for a down payment and closing costs. From then on it's all other people's money, the banks, and the tenants who pay for the investment. That's hard to beat in any business.

Real estate is one of the few businesses where the investor can virtually borrow almost all the money and go into business immediately. In addition, with real estate, that borrowed money is comparatively easy to find, is readily available, and uncomplicated to get.

The bank or seller provides the purchase money and then the tenants bring in the monthly rent check. These rent checks pay off the loan which increases your net worth. Not only does the rent pay off the loan, but it also pays for the interest, the taxes, insurance, and upkeep. Sometimes there's money leftover, and this is called positive cash flow—profit.

This phenomenon goes on every day, 365 days of the year. It's perpetuation merely depends on some good sound management skills on the part of the investor.

PROFIT THROUGH DEPRECIATION

Depreciation, the amount deducted for wear and tear on the property, is a tax write-off, or more succinctly put, it's pure profit for the investor.

As we all know, rarely does a property wear out nor is it used up, as is machinery in a factory. As a matter of fact, it more likely will appreciate in value. The history of real estate over the past 100 years proves this fact beyond a doubt.

This depreciation factor is truly a great financial benefit for the investor and shouldn't be overlooked or considered lightly. As far as I'm concerned, depreciation alone makes real estate as good an investment in the business world as there is.

Talk to any real estate investor and he'll tell you he doesn't pay income tax like others do. It's because he has a real estate depreciation tax write-off.

PROFIT THROUGH CAPITAL GROWTH

Once the cash flows through the business the investor is in a position to put those profits back into more property. Now, it's necessary to call to your attention that it might take a few years for profits to show up in an investment, but take my word for it, they will.

Putting these profits into more property is like oiling the perpetual money machine. Money invested in improvements increases the rents, which increases the value of the property, which increases the equity, which increases the borrowing power, which gives the investor the ability to buy more property or improve existing property, which starts the process all over again.

Add to this process one more important factor, and that is, each and every dollar invested back into the property provides another tax write-off, more depreciation, and more profit.

THE INVESTOR HAS THE FREEDOM TO CHOOSE

A benefit of real estate, unlike a lot of other businesses, gives the investor the ability to pick and choose the price and the amount of property that fits his investment program. The investor can pick from any sort of investment, all the way from a small, one-bedroom home to a duplex, four-plex, $100,000 properties, or if he is in a financial position to do so, $1,000,000 investments. Investment plans can be made by anyone regardless of age, financial net worth, or any other status in life.

Real estate provides a choice for the investor to reach a goal we all strive for—something called the great American Dream, the ability to live a secure, first-class life-style, with ease. There's no other way to put it. The average person can make it in real estate. As far as I can see, there's hardly any other way.

INDEPENDENCE AND FREEDOM

Not only is security important, and it is, but part of the reward of real estate ownership is the self-satisfaction of ownership. Along with that ownership is a business that provides freedom and independence.

Real Estate Is Not a Nine-to-Five Occupation

A successful and astute manager can come and go as he pleases. There's no time clock to punch and no boss to answer to. There's absolutely no threat of being fired or laid off when least expected.

That investor can hire management and have all the work done by others leaving him the job of depositing the money in the bank.

An investor can have a full-time occupation or profession and still invest in real estate. Real estate investing is the epitome of the entrepreneur, self-employed, free-enterprise methods of any person literally going from rags to riches.

Real Estate Is Guaranteed

Rarely will an investor lose money. Even with a loser, there's always something that's recoverable.

The secret is to keep the property in good condition, fully occupied with good tenants, and well-managed, and it becomes a guaranteed investment.

Real Estate Provides the Pride of a Job Well Done

There's also the added feature of fulfillment in doing a job and having done it well. This fulfillment is especially true of the small investor who has bought properties, improved and rejuvenated them, built them into a successful venture, and can look back and feel proud. That's a part of the enjoyment of owning real estate.

We can look at what we've done and say with pride, "I own that real estate; it's all mine." Quite frankly, that has a prestigious ring to it and raises one's position. There's admiration from the investor's peer group and others.

THE GOOSE THAT LAID THE GOLDEN EGG

We've talked throughout the book about the financial rewards. Let me tell you, they are there. There is an ultimate financial payoff. There comes a time, and it can happen more quickly with real estate than other businesses, when we can spend the egg check from the goose that laid the golden egg. That real estate egg check comes from

- Monthly rental income
- Contract for deed monthly payments
- Cash in the bank from sold property

Once the mortgages are paid, there's a steady cash flow coming from the perpetual money machine. It's money that's 100 percent spendable for the good things in life. This income, the wealth, and the net worth represents the ultimate security we've talked about in this book. It also represents independence.

PEACE OF MIND WITH FINANCIAL SECURITY

It's nice to view the majestic mountains or listen to the harmless pounding of the surf on a warm beach. But if we can't get there, it doesn't do much good.

It's also comforting to be able to go first class wherever and whenever we go, but if we can't afford it, first class will always be something we won't know.

As you well know, all these things come easy for the rich and famous. However, for those of us who've come up the hard way, I've found that real estate, and real estate alone, can and will provide a way to enjoy the good things in life.

THE LOVE OF LIFE IS THE RESULT

The ultimate goal of most of us is to enjoy the good things in life that are truly worthwhile.

Remember back when I told you to watch the pennies. By now those pennies should represent dollars. And if you've done the right thing, invested with prudence, with your real estate, there should be plenty of them. In fact, probably more than you realized, and more than you can handle.

But do you know something? There's no greater fulfillment than counting these dollars and then using them for life itself. I don't want to end this by sounding like a hedonist. I'm not. But I dare say, I've found more freedom, independence, and yes, religion, with the money earned from real estate than anyone can possibly measure.

Money, and making money, in itself is certainly not evil. There might be evil methods of making money in real estate, for example, being a slum landlord, or gouging the tenants, but these methods of making money are a waste of time and are unacceptable.

Money can, and will, increase our feeling of self-esteem and give us a feeling of well-being. We can talk all we want about the importance of faith, hope, charity, and love, but when it comes right down to it, there's the reality that money itself creates an atmosphere of our being able to appreciate and participate in these values, which can and will give us peace of mind.

Financial security can bring about the good things in our lives.

Index

Index

Edited by Nina E. Barr

Other Bestsellers From TAB

☐ **BECOMING SELF-EMPLOYED: HOW TO CREATE AN INDEPENDENT LIVELIHOOD—Susan Elliott**

If you've ever felt the urge to leave the corporate world to become your own boss, you'll want this book. It reveals what it's like to become successful, and what mistakes to avoid. Includes case studies of twenty successful entrepreneurs—what they did right, what they did wrong, and what they plan for the future and why. 160 pp., 19 illus.

Paper $7.95   **Book No. 30149**

☐ **HOW TO WRITE YOUR OWN WILL—John C. Howell**

Written by a nationally respected trial lawyer and corporate attorney with over 25 years experience, this invaluable book defines all the necessary terms, offers precise explanations for each type of will, and even relates the circumstances under which consultation with a lawyer is advisable. The necessary forms are clearly illustrated and easy to follow. Also presented are the methods of completely avoiding or minimizing the effect of probate. The instructions and documents discussed are in accordance with the statutes of all 50 states. 192 pp.

Paper $9.95   **Book No. 30137**

☐ **COACHING FOR IMPROVED WORK PERFORMANCE—Ferdinand F. Fournies**

Over 70,000 copies sold in hardcover; now available for the first time in paperback! By one of the nation's best-known business training consultants and specialist in coaching procedures, it shows you face-to-face coaching procedures that allow you to obtain immediate, positive results with your subordinates. Filled with examples, case studies, and practical problem-solving techniques. *a sorely needed guide/help book for sales-marketing managers to help them cope with their sales forces"*

                                    —The Sales Executive

224 pp., 6" × 9".
Paper $12.95   **Book No. 30054**

☐ **THE SMALL BUSINESS TAX ADVISOR: UNDERSTANDING THE NEW TAX LAW—Cliff Roberson, LLM, Ph.D**

The passage of the Tax Reform Act presented business and corporations with the most dramatic changes in tax laws and liabilities ever. Now, this thorough, easy-to-follow sourcebook provides the information you need to reduce your tax liability—while staying within the recently tightened guidelines! Writing especially for the small business, corporation, and stockholder, business law and tax expert Cliff Roberson gives you a practical overview of: All the new income tax rates. 176 pp., 6" × 9"

Paper $12.95   **Book No. 30024**

☐ **FORMING CORPORATIONS AND PARTNERSHIPS—John C. Howell**

If you're considering offering a service out of your home, buying a franchise, incorporating your present business, or starting a business venture of any type, you need this time- and money-saving guide. It explains the process of creating a corporation, gives information on franchising, the laws of partnership, and more. 192 pp., 5 1/2" × 8".

Paper $9.95   **Book No. 30143**

☐ **WINNING AT WORK: THE ROAD TO CAREER SUCCESS—Kenneth E. Norris**

The employee who knows the secret of "doing the little things well" gets ahead! Norris gives you important tips on: working with the boss toward making the company successful . . . mastering the art of making friends with other employees, especially those in important positions . . . developing a winning work philosophy . . . accomplishing work tasks without getting involved in administrative games . . . managing subordinates . . . and more. 126 pp.

Ha.d $14.95   **Book No. 30077**

☐ **THE ENTREPRENEUR'S GUIDE TO STARTING A SUCCESSFUL BUSINESS— James W. Halloran**

Here's a realistic approach to what it takes to start a small business, written by a successful entrepreneur and business owner. You'll learn step-by-step every phase of a business start-up from getting the initial idea to realizing a profit. Included is advice on: designing a store layout, pricing formulas and strategies, advertising and promotion, and more. 256 pp.

Paper $15.95   **Book No. 30049**

☐ **UNDERSTANDING WALL STREET—2nd Edition—Jeffrey B. Little and Lucien Rhodes**

This bestselling guide to understanding and investing on Wall Street has been completely updated to reflect the most current developments in the stock market. The substantial growth of mutual funds, the emergence of index options, the sweeping new tax bill, and how to keep making money even after the market reaches record highs and lows are a few of the things explained in this long-awaited revision. 240 pp., illustrated.

Paper $9.95   **Hard $19.95**
Book No. 30020

Other Bestsellers From TAB

☐ **EVERYDAY LAW FOR EVERYONE—John C. Howell**

Everyday Law for Everyone explains everything the average citizen needs to know to confidently handle a variety of common legal problems. By following this guide you will be able to: write your own will, change your name, win landlord/tenant disputes, set up partnerships, avoid a probate, adopt a child, form your own corporation, and draw up business contracts—without the expense of complications of hiring a lawyer! *Everyday Law for Everyone* presents the facts about our legal system. A number of legal forms and documents that you can use in specific situations, or refer to when writing your own are included. By doing some of the work yourself, you can save on costly legal fees. Knowledge is your greatest defense! With this laymen's guide, you can be in a controlling position when the unexpected happens. 238 pp.

Paper $9.95   **Book No. 30011**

☐ **THE PERSONAL TAX ADVISOR: UNDERSTANDING THE NEW TAX LAW—Cliff Roberson, LLM, Ph.D**

If the new federal tax law has left you puzzled as to how it will affect your taxes, this sourcebook will make it all amazingly clear. It simplifies the massive three-volume, 2800-page tax law into language the average taxpayer can understand. There's a personal tax calendar listing important tax dates, a deductions checklist, and advice on preparing for a tax audit. Major areas examined include: permissible deductions, non-real estate investments, fringe benefits, record keeping requirements, real estate, tax shelters, pensions, and tax audits. 176 pp., 6" × 9", Paperback.

Paper $12.95   **Book No. 3013**

Send $1 for the new TAB Catalog describing over 1300 titles currently in print and receive a coupon worth $1 off on your next purchase from TAB.

(Pa. residents add 6% sales tax. NY residents add sales tax. Orders outside U.S. must be prepaid with international money orders in U.S. dollars.)

Prices subject to change without notice.

To purchase these or any other books from TAB, visit your local bookstore, return this coupon, or call toll-free 1-800-233-1128 (In PA and AK call 1-717-794-2191).

Product No.	Hard or Paper	Title	Quantity	Price

☐ Check or money order enclosed made payable to TAB BOOKS Inc.

Charge my   ☐ VISA   ☐ MasterCard   ☐ American Express

Acct. No. _____ Exp. _____

Signature _____

Please Print
Name _____

Company _____

Address _____

City _____

State _____ Zip _____

Subtotal	
Postage/Handling ($5.00 outside U.S.A. and Canada)	$2.50
In PA add 6% sales tax	
TOTAL	

Mail coupon to:

TAB BOOKS Inc.
Blue Ridge Summit
PA 17294-0840   BC